THE BLACK ATHLETE:

HIS STORY IN AMERICAN HISTORY

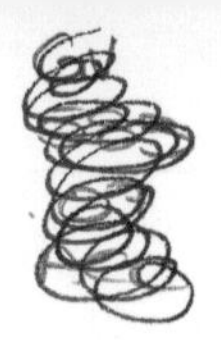

THE BLACK ATHLETE:

HIS STORY IN AMERICAN HISTORY

BY JACK ORR

INTRODUCTION BY JACKIE ROBINSON

Publishers, New York

For Sonny

All photos courtesy of United Press International

21 West 38th Street, New York, New York 10018
Published simultaneously in Canada by George J. McLeod Ltd.
73 Bathurst Street, Toronto 2B, Ontario
Printed and bound in the United States of America
Library of Congress Catalog Card Number: 69-17728

CONTENTS

PREFACE

All I ask is that you respect me as a human being. I am proud to be a black. I am not ashamed of my dark skin. God has given us certain unique qualities and we cherish them just as Englishmen, Frenchmen, Jews, Indians and every other group of common origin cherish theirs . . .

Jackie Robinson

This book is about sports in America and the role the Afro-American has played in its development. The odds against him have always been overwhelming, the struggle often painful and ugly, the rewards sometimes gratifying. It is a battle that continues today. For, though many of the obstacles placed in the path of the black athlete over the years have been knocked down, many others remain standing. These are the targets being aimed at by men of good will, white and black. This book will trace the part Afro-Americans have taken in the sports and games of the country and will try to show what might come about in the continuing struggle. The fight against bigotry and discrimination in sports is no different from the fight for freedom being waged by all blacks.

Sports has had a hold on America since the earliest Colonial times. Though the seventeenth century was a grim period of struggling just to survive for the white settlers, they found time to introduce competitive games into their lives. But as happened in so many other areas of American life, Afro-Americans never got a fair shake.

The reason in the beginning, of course, was that they were slaves. At the time the white settlers were breaking the land, the first shiploads of blacks were arriving in Virginia from West Africa. They were sent into the field to harvest the tobacco and rice crops. In the Southern states slavery was sanctioned by law and out of the prosperity on which it was based, the plantation system grew and with it, the creation of a leisure class. The owners of these great plantations bred thoroughbred horses and raced them against each other for heavy wagers.

It was only natural that the dirty and often dangerous work of grooming, feeding, breaking, exercising and training horses should be delegated to the slaves. They also became the jockeys for the plantation-vs.-plantation match races. Thus, the blacks who carried their plantations' colors aboard the horses (and often into the boxing ring) actually were the earliest professional athletes. They competed throughout this country and in Europe and a few were given their freedom after making a great deal of money for their owners.

But as the years passed, it became increasingly difficult for the black athlete in any sport to receive recognition. He suffered punishing trials for almost three hundred years. It is only perhaps in the last three decades that gains have been made. In many ways, the progress has been enormous. In baseball, football, boxing, track and field and basketball, the color line has been so completely cracked that blacks place at the very top of any list of super-stars.

Today every big league professional club in a major sport has Afro-Americans on its roster.* The result has been far-reaching and wholesome. Thousands of blacks have achieved personal fulfillment, college educations and wealth. Millions of blacks have been able to cheer for their heroes and have been inspired by them. Millions of whites, too, who are impressed by a man who can win a ball game or a fight, have been educated by what they have seen of black athletes in arenas and on television.

The story of the late Branch Rickey, who broke organized baseball's seemingly impenetrable color line by bringing in Jackie Robinson a little over twenty years ago, perhaps shows how far the country has come.

Rickey was coach of the Ohio Wesleyan University baseball team, even though he was only twenty-two. One of his players, Charlie Thomas, was black. Rickey took special care of Thomas and went out of his way to protect him from rebuffs from teammates or opponents.

One time the team was playing South Bend, Indiana, during the 1904 season, and when the players checked in to the Oliver Hotel, a frightened hotel manager halted the incoming team in the lobby. He said that the black boy could not go upstairs. Rickey sent his student manager to the Y.M.C.A. to look for a vacancy.

"Maybe it would be better if I went back home," Thomas said.

"No," Rickey said. "We'll be all right."

Rickey persuaded the hotel manager to let Thomas wait upstairs in Branch's own room. There the big athlete broke down. His 220-pound body hunched over in a gesture that Rickey never forgot. As Thomas rubbed hard from wrist to finger tips, tears from his grimacing face splashed against his large hands.

"Black skin . . ." he murmured in a half sob. "Black skin . . . Oh, if I could only make 'em white."

Forty-three years later, as he courageously challenged baseball's unwritten law—for whites only—and made Jackie Robinson a big leaguer, Rickey said he still remembered that picture of big Thomas trying to change the color of his skin.

Jack Orr

*With the exception of hockey. The reason for this is that the overwhelming majority of big league players are of Canadian origin and the proportion of blacks in Canada is minute. At this writing, there are several Afro-Americans in the minors; some will probably make their debut in two or three years.

INTRODUCTION

THE RIGHT OF EVERY AMERICAN to first-class citizenship is the most important issue of our times. That is why we, of black ancestry, fight for that right. We have no illusions about the difficulties that lie ahead. We know that bigots intend to go on fighting us and will continue to use the big lie that we are inferior based solely on skin color. We know that no matter how far we progress the lie will still be there. We know that this lie must be exposed and destroyed if America is to survive. We know our stake in America is great and the future is bright for black children as well as white. That is why we continue to fight.

In this book, Jack Orr has traced the history of the black athlete in America. It is an intriguing story. My part in it is incidental. But the book shows how far we, who happened to have been black, have traveled. From a time when we were considered toadying playthings we have progressed to the point where a great many of the best fighters, the best ballplayers and the best runners and jumpers are black—and are so acknowledged in our country.

More important than this, however, is the struggle all of our black people are undergoing to take their real place in society. It is hoped that this book will help in that struggle.

Jackie Robinson

Jackie Robinson, Montreal Club, 1946

ACKNOWLEDGMENTS

In compiling this work, the author leaned on many friends and one-time colleagues on newspapers and magazines, in broadcasting and in the sports business. Among them were:

Robert Lipsyte and Leonard Koppett of *The New York Times;* Milton Gross and Larry Merchant of the *New York Post;* Stan Isaacs of *Newsday;* Sam Lacy of the *Afro-American* newspapers; Sandy Grady of the *Philadelphia Bulletin* and Jack Hand of the Associated Press.

Others were Lee Allen of Baseball's Hall of Fame in Cooperstown, New York; Joe Reichler of the Baseball Commissioner's Office; Nat Fleischer, editor of *Ring;* Al Silverman at *Sport* Magazine; Andy Crichton at *Sports Illustrated,* and writers Roger Kahn and Dick Schaap.

Joe Bostic and Sam Chase of Station WLIB in Harlem were helpful, as were Herb Goren and Heywood Hale Broun, CBS; Joe Garagiola, Joe Gallagher and Bob Cunniff, NBC; Harold Rosenthal, American Football League; Jim Heffernan, National Football League; C. Robert Paul, U.S. Olympic Committee, and Pat Lynch, Thoroughbred Racing Association.

Files of *The Sporting News,* published by C. C. Johnson Spink, were invaluable, and the author is also indebted to the patient and cooperative attendants at the famed Schomburg Collection of the New York Public Library, in Harlem.

I am also grateful for the assistance afforded by Lion Press publishers Gordon Saks and Robert Fenton; by my editor, Mrs. Patricia Murray, and by Mrs. Angelika Wolff, who was copy editor.

CHAPTER I

"They're Off!"

American colonists began to look for diversions from the rigor of everyday life as soon as they achieved even a small amount of leisure time. They had horses, men and the time, so it was natural that they would turn to racing thoroughbreds. Racing dated back to the twelfth century in England, and many of the new Americans recalled it with delight.

As early as the seventeenth century, not long after the first ship loads of blacks had arrived from West Africa, the colonists began racing horses. They turned over the job of training them to their slaves, and the blacks became so knowledgeable in the peculiar ways of thoroughbreds that black jockeys and trainers became the toasts of the American turf world.

The early races were all match affairs, with heavy wagering between owners and partisans of sectional favorites. Descriptions of some of these matches have been passed down but always the jockeys bore names like "Pompey," "Scipio," "Cato" and "Caesar." It was the custom among slave owners of that period to air their knowledge of the classics by bestowing the names of great Romans upon their chattels.

This kind of match held sway until the start of the Civil War. There were attempts to set up organized racing in Virginia, Maryland and Kentucky, but the first thoroughbred racing meet in the country was held at the Saratoga Springs, New York, track in 1863. Belmont Park in Long Island, New York, opened three years later. Black jockeys, expert by now in training and riding, came along. One black rider on record was known only by the name of "Abe." In the inaugural Jerome Handicap at Belmont, he won with a horse named Watson, and he followed that by winning the first Travers Stakes at Saratoga with Merrill.

Isaac Murphy, whose record of three Kentucky Derby wins was unbeaten for forty years

Churchill Downs, at Louisville, Kentucky, opened its track in 1875, and the first Kentucky Derby was held that year. Of the fifteen jockeys in that first Derby, fourteen were blacks and their names did not appear in the program. One of the blacks, Oliver Lewis, stepped down with the winner, Aristides. The distance was a mile-and-a-half, instead of the mile-and-a-quarter of today, and the time of 2:37 3/4 was the fastest ever run by a three-year-old in America until then. Today the world record for that distance is 2:26.

Other black trainers and jockeys made their mark in this beginning period. Trainer James Williams saddled the 1876 Derby winner, Vagrant. Trainer Ed (Brown Dick) Brown and jockey Billy Walker won the next year with Baden-Baden. Walker was also up on Ten Broeck when he won (by ten lengths) a two-mile match race against a California mare, Mollie McCarthy. Garrison Lewis won the 1880 Derby; Babe Hurd won the classic in 1882. A former jockey, Raleigh Colston, trained Leonatus, winner in 1883.

But the outstanding horse rider of the period was the Afro-American Isaac Murphy. He won immortality by winning three Kentucky Derbies, a record that stood for forty years, until tied by Earl Sande in 1930. Later, the record was beaten by Eddie Arcaro who won five Derbies (1938, 1941, 1945, 1948, 1952). In this generation, also, Bill Hartack won four, Willie Shoemaker, three.

Born in Lexington, Kentucky, on January 1, 1861 (interestingly, the date—January 1—is recognized as the birthday of all thoroughbreds), Murphy won his first race at the age of fourteen in 1875. He was acknowledged as a superior rider in subsequent years. He rode the first four winners of the Latonia Derby and took the American Derby at Washington Park in four of its first five runnings.

He was twenty-nine when he won a thrilling match race against the great Snapper Garrison, the jockey for whom "garrison finish" was coined. Murphy was up on Salvator; Garrison's mount was Tenny. The match between the two peerless riders was as much a magnet as the horses and a record throng from New York and Philadelphia turned out at Sheepshead Bay, New York. Garrison, trailing all the way to the home stretch, gave Tenny his celebrated finishing rush, but Murphy held on aboard Salvator to win by a head. A colored lithograph of the race was used as an advertisement by a champagne company and for a decade adorned New York saloons.

Murphy died in Lexington in 1896. Sixty years later he was elected to racing's Hall of Fame as the outstanding jockey of his time.

Another great jockey of the period was Jimmy Winkfield, who won the Kentucky Derby in 1902 on a colt, Alan-a-Dale. The opposition included a stable mate, Rival, a renowned colt named Abe Frank and another named Inventor.

The huge Churchill Downs crowd was astonished to see Winkfield take Alan-a-Dale to the front almost immediately at a pace more suited to a seven-furlong race than to the Derby's mile-and-a-quarter. He raced the half in 48, a scorching pace, and the rest of the field straggled behind. Now on the home stretch, Abe Frank dropped out, and Inventor, less highly regarded but still a good colt, closed speedily. It was a wild stretch run and a wilder finish, but the able Winkfield, riding with hands and heels, held off the challenger to win by a neck.

Other expert black riders followed. One was the outstanding Monk Overton, who rode six winners out of six mounts at Washington Park in 1891. John Stoval and Pike Barnes each had scored four-for-four, but Overton's performance stood as an all-time record for sixteen years until duplicated by Jimmy Lee in 1907.

The first black jockey to win international acclaim was Willie Simms. After winning the Kentucky Derby twice, in 1896 and 1898, he went to England where he became the first American jockey to win an event on an English course with an American horse, owned and trained by Americans. Upon his return, Simms was cheered by all as one of the true turf heroes.

Winkfield, who had done such a heroic job with Alan-a-Dale, had another Derby on his record and was shooting for three in a row in 1903 when he made a costly mistake. His mount, named Early, was lengths in front going into the stretch and Winkfield decided to coast home. A horse named Judge Himes came with a roar in the stretch and nipped the napping Winkfield at the wire. His 1902 Derby was the last won by a black rider. He later rode in France and won the renowned Prix du Président de la République Stake at St. Cloud as late as 1923.

The last black jockey to have a mount in the Derby was Jess Conley. He finished third on Colston in 1911. Since then, the track has seen some good riders, Charlie Gregg, R. Simpson, Johnny Hudgins, Clarence Reed and C. Dishmon. But old-timers say they were handicapped because they did not have the opportunities offered black riders before the turn of the century.

Some of those outstanding jockeys of old were Lonnie Clayton, Soup Perkins, Billy Mitchell, Linc Jones, Tommy Knight, Spider Anderson, Jerry Chorn, William Porter, Tom Britton and Bob (Tiny) Williams.

For some reason, Afro-Americans held on to their jobs in riding steeplechase horses. It is a more dangerous way of life, of course, and possibly white riders were glad to let blacks do the jumping. George and Charlie Smoot were remarkably able jump riders, and the latter was the leading steeplechase rider in 1927, with ten winners out of fifty-three mounts. As late as 1936, Paul McGinnis led with nine winners out of twenty-eight mounts.

Of more recent vintage, the track has seen G. Cardoza, R. Holland, Al Brown and Raymond Booker, but the black jockey has been by-passed in recent years in favor of Central and South Americans.

Track officials claim that blacks have grown themselves out of the profession of riding horses. "There just aren't proportionate black jockeys any longer," one official said. "Remember, blacks have been here in the United States longer than most of the rest of us. Everybody has grown. There are fewer white jockeys, too. The affluent society has taken away our black riders."

Many track buffs say the track suffered a great loss when it began passing up black riders. They say the black riders of the past had an incomparable flair, which is lacking in the current racing world.

Jockey Jimmy Winkfield wins the Prix du Président de la République, France, 1923

CHAPTER II

"8-9-10-Out!"

Perhaps the single most dramatic moment in the history of sports in this country came on the night of June 22, 1938, at Yankee Stadium in New York City. That was the night the immortal Joe Louis, who had recently become heavyweight champion of the world, explosively knocked out the German challenger, Max Schmeling, in a little over two minutes as 70,000 fans screamed their approval and millions of others hunched excitedly over their radio sets.

To set the scene for this unforgettable fight, it must be recalled that Louis, who had been fighting professionally for four years and was still only twenty-four, had won every fight of his career—except a previous bout with Schmeling in 1936. At the time of the return match, Adolf Hitler was at the height of his power in Germany and the United States was beginning to be seriously disturbed over his teachings that the Germans were a "master race," destined to rule the world. The Nazis, and Schmeling himself, voiced particular disdain for blacks in general and Joe Louis in particular. Schmeling called him a "black, stupid amateur."

Throughout the world the bout took on international and racial implications—American democracy vs. Nazism and Aryan supremacy. Schmeling, a powerful puncher and very durable on defense, was favored by the experts. They had seen the German dynamite Joe Louis into submission two years earlier and had not forgotten. They forecast an early knockout of Louis, and it was hard for anybody to foresee that they would be wrong.

On that hot night in 1938, Louis was a dedicated and ferocious fighter. At the first bell he dashed from his corner and caught Schmeling with a

June 22, 1938 . . . the historic Louis-Schmeling fight

quick left followed by a punishing right cross. The German went down, and the crowd exploded with deafening cheers. He got up, blood trickling from his mouth. Louis hit him again, a left and a right. Schmeling actually whimpered in pain as he went down again. His face had an anguished look. He tried to get up, but the battle was over. Louis wore an almost disinterested look as the referee counted to ten.

Louis was to continue his domination of all boxing for the next ten years. He was probably the most popular black athlete. He not only won the acclaim of his own people, but he also changed the image of the Afro-American in the eyes of millions around the world.

He was to be followed by other great black ring champions, of course, and there had been some before him, but those two minutes on that June night in 1938, represented, without a doubt, the height of black boxing achievement. Louis successfully defended his title an unprecedented twenty-five times and retired undefeated as champ in 1949. Later, he tried unsuccessfully to come back and quit for good in 1951, when he was thirty-seven.

Long before Louis, blacks were playing important roles in boxing. In the earliest days, just as jockey-slaves rode horses for their masters, black fighters carried their owners' colors into the ring.

Records are naturally fragmentary, but it is known that outstanding pugilists of various sections and plantations were pitted against each other, with a good deal of wagering going on about the outcome. Gradually boxing spread northward and many blacks who had become freemen continued to follow fighting careers.

One of the first was Bill Richmond, born at Staten Island, New York, in 1763. He was a light heavyweight by current standards, standing five feet, nine inches tall and weighing 175 pounds. But he took on all comers, and held his own against men weighing as much as fifty pounds more. Richmond was taken to England in 1777 by General Earl Percy, a commander of British forces then occupying New York. The lithe black fighter had won several bouts with British soldiers in matches arranged by General Percy for the amusement of his friends.

In England, Richmond ran off a series of impressive victories and was hired by Lord Camelford, a nobleman and sports fan. The Lord backed the American heavily, hired him as his valet and later helped him establish a hotel in Haymarket, which was highly patronized by the nobility and gentry. Richmond even drew mention in the journals of Lord Byron, the poet. He was also idolized by the working class. He continued to fight until he was fifty-seven years old, knocking out one Jack Carter in three rounds. Richmond died in 1829, at the age of sixty-six, and he was greatly mourned, historians of the time tell us, by his fans of all classes.

Another Afro-American was Tom Molyneux, born a slave in 1784, in Georgetown, South Carolina. His father and his grandfather before him had been notable boxers among the plantation slaves.

One story tells how Molyneux, in bondage to the Southern family of that name, earned his freedom by defeating a bully from a neighboring Virginia plantation. He made his way to New York City and made his headquarters the old Catherine Markets. There, he challenged and defeated all comers. Next, he caught on with a merchant ship crew and went to England, where the fight game was flourishing. Molyneux, who weighed 185, was an instant success. He smashed out eight consecutive victories over British fighters, all of them fighting under the name, "Unknown," because they feared they would lose "social prestige," if it became known that they had fought a black.

Soon the British were getting excited over the American. They enthusiastically turned out for his fights and set up a cry for a bout between the black and the recognized world heavyweight title holder, the Englishman, Tom Cribb. The bout, billed as the first "Fight of the Century," finally was arranged. Odds heavily favored the American challenger.

More than 20,000 fans attended the match, and it was a grueling one. Molyneux was getting far the better of it, punching Cribb almost at will. But in the twenty-third round, with Cribb groggy and unable to continue in the allocated time limit, his seconds claimed that a foul had been committed. The recess permitted Cribb time to recover, though the fight should have been ended there.

In the thirty-first round, Molyneux flattened Cribb with a right-hand blow. But in trying to get out of Cribb's falling way, Molyneux stumbled, lost his balance and tumbled into a ring post with such force that he fractured his skull. Both men were revived for the thirty-second round and were shoved into the ring, where they staggered around on unsteady feet, both falling down as the round ended. In the next round, Cribb smashed Molyneux in the face with all his strength and the first interracial title bout in history was over.

Molyneux never recovered from that injury. Later, he had a rematch with Cribb and was knocked out in eleven rounds, after suffering a broken jaw in the tenth. Though he was befriended by Bill Richmond, Molyneux went downhill swiftly and died at the age of thirty-four in 1818.

It should be noted that these early fights were all bare-knuckle events under a code called the "London Prize Ring Rules." Basically, they prohibited the hitting of an opponent while he was down, seizing him by the hair or breeches or any part below the waist—but almost everything else went. Padded gloves were not introduced until 1865, when the Marquis of Queensberry instituted his set of rules. Bare-knuckle fighting continued in America even after the Marquis of Queensberry revisions, the last bout being held on July 8, 1889, between John L. Sullivan and Jake Kilrain. Thereafter, no bare-knuckle championship fight was held.

Many notable black fighters followed Richmond and Molyneux. Bob Smith, born in 1840, in Washington, D.C., lived in Liverpool, England, and won many important ring contests in his day. Another black, Bob

West Indian Peter Jackson, "the Prince of Fighters," is remembered as a pioneer in boxing

Travers, was said to have fought more bouts in the late nineteenth century than any other fighter till that time. Then there was George Godfrey, of Boston, Mass., the first heavyweight champion among Afro-Americans. Once he was matched with John L. Sullivan, but Sullivan never risked his title in a match with a black and the bout was canceled. Charles Hadley, of Bridgeport, Connecticut, established an impressive record, but Sullivan would not fight him, either.

Peter Jackson was undoubtedly one of the great heavyweight fighters of all time. Along with Bill Richmond, Jackson is enshrined in boxing's Hall of Fame as a member of "the pioneer group," who set a pace for the game. Born in the West Indies in 1861, he was a handsome man who stood six-feet-one and weighed 212. They called him "the Prince of Fighters" because of his flawless, cat-like style and his proud, challenging poise.

As a seaman, Jackson arrived in Sydney, Australia—a twenty-two-year-old novice pugilist. He worked enormously hard with a professional boxing teacher named Larry Foley. Three years later he won the championship of Australia by defeating Tom Lees in thirty rounds. In 1888, Jackson came to the United States, arriving in San Francisco. He fought the Afro-American champion, George Godfrey, and beat him in nineteen rounds. Then he conquered a promising young heavyweight, Joe McAuliffe. His next match was with Patsy Cardiff, of San Francisco, whose claim to fame was a six-round draw with the champion, John L. Sullivan. Jackson put him away easily in ten rounds.

Sullivan still drew the color line and many of the other ranking heavyweights did too, so there was little chance for Jackson. He went to England and knocked out a highly publicized British prospect, Jem Smith, in two rounds.

Back in America, he was signed to meet the up-and-coming James J. Corbett. It was youth vs. age, even though Corbett was conceding thirty-six pounds to Jackson. But the white man was already a polished fighter and a superb ring strategist. Jackson had more power. The match was a natural and a purse of $10,000, very substantial for the time, was posted.

When the gong rang, Jackson leaped across the ring as if to finish Corbett off quickly. Corbett back-pedaled, dodged and boxed. Jackson pursued him, looking for his one shot that would end the fight. But though in the sixteenth round Jackson finally caught Corbett with a powerful blow to the side, Corbett was able to hold Jackson off until he had shaken off the effect of the blow. The fight rolled on, round after round, and from the thirtieth on, both men were tired and showed it. After the fortieth round, it was evident that the battle was merely a contest in endurance. After sixty rounds, both men were so exhausted they could hardly meet at the center of the ring. The referee called the fight "no contest," and canceled all bets—after four hours of rugged fighting.

Jackson had other good fights. He won the British Empire heavyweight title in 1892, became an actor for a while, returned to the ring when he was almost forty years old and lost several times. He died in 1901.

There were blacks fighting in other divisions, fine fighters many of them. But often they were the victims of discrimination and exploitation, and this drove them to fight in other countries.

George Dixon, born in Halifax, Nova Scotia, was the first black to win the world bantamweight and world featherweight titles. He was called "Little Chocolate," and was a flashy showman. He dressed stylishly and traveled around the country, meeting all comers and posting substantial forfeits to guarantee knockouts or decisive decisions within four rounds. When Dixon was at his prime, he wrote an autobiography, in which he estimated he fought more than 500 bouts to that time, adding "I have won or drawn in every one of these contests in which I have engaged with two exceptions . . ." In all, Dixon fought more than 800 times in a 20-year career.

"Little Chocolate," George Dixon, who fought 800 matches during his 20-year career

Some historians say there never has been an equal to George Dixon in fighting talent. He was named to boxing's Hall of Fame some years ago. His perfect timing and skills in punching, blocking and evading blows were historic and won him a popularity not unlike that which greeted Sugar Ray Robinson half a century later. Dixon married a white woman and it caused no untoward comment, remarkable for that day and age.

The next to make history was the lightweight Joe Gans. The division limit at that time was 133 pounds, raised in 1909 to 135. And though Gans held the lightweight title from 1901 to 1908, he fought anyone at any weight. His endurance was remarkable and once he fought three men in one day, on July 15, 1901.

He compiled a strong record even before taking the lightweight title from Frank Erne by knocking the champion cold in the first round. New York City still was closed ground to black fighters in those days, so Gans did most of his fighting on the road.

Gans was challenged for the title by Battling Nelson, a hard-hitting, rugged Dane. Their first fight has been passed down through the years as a classic in fistic history. The bout was scheduled for forty-five rounds and for forty-two of those rounds, Gans side-stepped, jabbed and counter-punched the oncoming Nelson. Some observers said that Gans had won every round when the forty-second started. But when Nelson staggered back wildly under a flurry of jabs and hooks, he fouled the black so obviously and viciously that the referee stopped the fight and awarded the title to the champion. That was something unusual in those days, particularly in a title fight, but there was little else the official could do.

Gans kept busy for two more years before giving Nelson another shot at the crown. This time they met in San Francisco on July 4, 1908. Even though, by this time, Joe Gans was thirty-four, a shell of his old self and racked by tuberculosis, it took the rugged yellow-headed Nelson seventeen rounds before he could register a knockout. Gans died two years later in Prescott, Arizona.

Lightweight Joe Gans, renowned for his remarkable endurance

There were many other prominent black fighters of the period. Joe Walcott, the original whose name the latter-day heavyweight adopted, was from Toronto and punched his way to the welterweight title. But like Gans, he fought all comers, including heavyweights. Walcott had tremendous hitting strength and moved well.

Once Walcott, who stood only five feet, one-and-a-half inches and weighed 142 pounds, took on a 200-pound heavyweight, Joe Choynski, in San Francisco. Choynski's claim to renown was that he had fought a twenty-round draw with the great Jim Jeffries. Walcott knocked out Choynski in seven rounds. Later, Walcott offered to put up $5,000 to back a bout with Jeffries. The money would go to Jeffries, Walcott said, if this statement were proved untrue: "that James J. Jeffries cannot stop me in six rounds." He added that he was ready at any time to fight Jeffries for six or ten rounds to a decision. They never fought.

Joe Jeannette, Sam McVey, Sam Langford and Harry Wills are other names which deserve mention in this era. They ran into the color line many times and champions feared to fight them. As a result, they were often matched against each other; Jeannette fighting Langford ten times and Wills fighting Langford fourteen times, for instance.

Joe Walcott, welterweight champion who once challenged the great Jim Jeffries with $5,000 of his own money

Jack Johnson was the first black world heavyweight champion. He was also the most colorful, most independent, most confident, most flamboyant non-conformist who ever laced on a glove. He was magnetic, dynamic and controversial. And he may have been the best heavyweight fighter of all time.

Born in Galveston, Texas, in 1878, Johnson grew into a magnificently muscled young man. His fight weight was 195 and he stood a shade over six feet. His head was shaven skin clean, and his face was strong, sturdy and well fleshed, but his nose was flat and broad. He almost immediately became a contender of consequence, but champions gave him the run-around. He had to fight eighty times over a five-year period before he was given a shot at the title, then held by Tommy Burns. Burns began a world tour, with Jack Johnson right on his heels, issuing challenges at every stop. Finally, near Sydney, Australia, on December 26, 1908, Burns accepted the challenge—and Johnson masterfully knocked him out in the fourteenth round.

Back in the United States, Johnson, a high-living man, began cashing in on his fame. He had married a white woman, bought a huge flashy wardrobe and the biggest car on the market, and was living in high fashion, indeed. He had three no-decision bouts before taking on Stanley Ketchel, the middleweight champion, in a bout that is historic. Ketchel, weighing only 160 pounds, made the mistake of trying to knock out Johnson with a haymaker in the twelfth round. Johnson went down, but was up at the count of eight. Ketchel waded in excitedly to follow up his advantage, but Johnson, ever the defensive master, was ready, and as Ketchel leaped in, the first black heavyweight champ met him with a wicked left to the jaw and followed with a right and another left. Ketchel was on his back, out cold, for a long time.

By this time there was general griping about Johnson's behavior. A cry went up for America to find a white challenger who could beat Johnson. But there was a shortage of white hopes in that era, so the pressure was put on old Jim Jeffries, the ex-champ, by then thirty-five, to come out of retirement and meet Johnson. Tex Rickard promoted the bout in Reno, Nevada, on July 4, 1910, under a blazing sun. It was no contest. Johnson's superiority was obvious immediately. He kidded with ringsiders, made asides to Jeffries, chatted with the referee. Then Jack began shooting in long snake-like left jabs and some swift uppercuts. Jeffries couldn't cope. In the fifteenth, Johnson shuffled toward Jim, sent a burning left to his jaw and knocked him down for the first time in his career. He arose just at the count of ten, and Johnson hit him in the same place. Jeffries sank to the floor for the full count.

There followed a spree of world-wide celebration for Johnson. He was fêted by white and black all around the world. He ran into trouble with the law over his association with white women. Congress went so far as to make it a federal offense to transport the Johnson fight pictures in commerce. He went into exile, first in Paris, then in Barcelona. He opened a café and went broke and when he was offered a fight with Jess Willard in Havana, Cuba, he took it. That fight ended with Johnson "knocked out" in the twenty-sixth round, but pictures showed him on his back with a gloved hand up shielding his eyes from the sun. Many eyewitnesses and experts say that Jack threw the fight to Willard as part of an arrangement whereby he would be freed from entanglement with the law. Other eyewitnesses insist that Johnson was beaten fairly.

Criticism of Jack Johnson's behavior outside of the ring undoubtedly was based on the color of his skin. There were white champions, then and later, who were less than models of decorum and modesty. But Johnson's era was marked by persecution of blacks in general and the world was not ready for him. One fight writer who still remembers has called him "a combination of Cassius Clay, Sonny Liston, Sugar Ray Robinson and Maxie Rosenbloom—all personalities loaded with color and magnetism." Another writer has said: "If Jack Johnson had been a white man, he would have attained an influence in the world which few other men ever attained." If he was individualistic and erratic, he was also gentlemanly, courteous and humane. He fought a charity bout with Sam Langford, all proceeds going to the victims of the San Francisco earthquake. He actually wept when he knocked out the once great but aged Bob Fitzsimmons as part of his campaign to win the title. "It was pitiful," Johnson said, "and I do not take much credit to myself, but it seemed necessary at the time."

Inside the ring, everybody agreed, Johnson was superb. He was a master boxer, with an almost perfect defense and a smashing wallop. He fought flatfooted, shuffling around the ring rather awkwardly, which concealed the real speed of his movements. He never allowed himself to be hurried, conserving his resources of strength until the time came for the kill.

Johnson was always accessible to a challenger, and besides Fitzsimmons, Ketchel, Burns and Jeffries, he put away top-notchers such as Sam Langford, Sam McVey, Joe Jeannette and Jim Flynn. He held the title of heavyweight champion of the world longer than anyone, save Joe Louis. And though he fought some of the hardest hitters of his day, he left the rink unmarked and unscarred.

Probably the greatest honor to come Jack Johnson's way was bestowed eight years after he died following an automobile accident in 1946. That was the year boxing's Hall of Fame was founded. Johnson was one of the first installed. Nat Fleischer, the authoritative ring historian, has named Johnson the all-time number one heavyweight champion, three rungs above Jack Dempsey and five rungs above Joe Louis.

After Johnson lost his crown in 1915, there was a twenty-two year wait before another black won it. To be sure, a few blacks in other divisions climbed to the top. The clever Tiger Flowers won the welterweight crown from Harry Greb in 1926. Battling Siki, born in a West African jungle, won the French Croix de Guerre in World War I, and knocked out Georges Carpentier, the idol of France, for the light heavyweight title in 1923.

Jack Johnson—the great black world heavyweight champion

Sam Langford, the Boston Tar Baby, was another outstanding fighter, whose career spread between 1902 and 1923. He won 150 of his 250 fights, but never had a chance at the title. And the giant black, Harry Wills, perhaps the most masterful boxer after Jack Johnson, never was able to get the reigning champion, Jack Dempsey, into a ring. The feeling that Johnson had somehow made all blacks suspect persisted through sport's golden age, and promoters, though they knew Wills as the most outstanding challenger of the time, made no secret of their ban.

Between 1915 and 1937 no black heavyweight was given the opportunity to wrest the title from the white champions. When one finally was allowed a shot at the crown, he was to be one of the genuine sports heroes of all time and he was to usher in an era in which black fighters all but dominated the game of fist-fighting. His name was Joe Louis.

Middleweight Stanley Ketchel and Jack Johnson spar before their historic bout

Ketchel (above left) and Johnson pose for reporters before their fight

CHAPTER III

The Brown Bomber Leads the Way

Joseph Louis Barrow was born the son of a sharecropper on a farm near Lafayette, Alabama, May 13, 1914. He was the fifth of seven offspring, and as a child of four he worked in the cotton fields. He did not learn to read until he was nine. When he was twelve his widowed mother and stepfather moved the brood to Detroit and he became a ragamuffin of the streets. He toted ice for fly-by-night icemen to earn a few pennies and began learning his trade of boxing in gang fights in the heart of what was called Detroit's "Black Bottom," a ghetto of the period.

Soon he was fighting as an amateur with almost immediate success. He pounded his way to the national amateur light heavyweight championship when he was still not twenty years old. In two years as an amateur, he won forty-three fights by knockouts and seven by decision, lost only four (at least three of them by debatable decisions) and caught the eye of two Detroit blacks, John Roxborough and Julian Black. They led him cautiously into the professional ranks. Louis was thus the first black fighter of stature to be managed by blacks. Another black, Marshall Miles, handled him later in his career. His trainer was Jack Blackburne, a former black fighter.

Joe learned quickly. His handlers not only polished his fighting style, but they also taught him to comport himself with dignity. The ban against blacks in boxing, erected in Jack Johnson's day, still haunted Afro-American athletes. Blackburne, who had been through it, muttered darkly, "They ain't never gonna let another colored boy wear that crown."

Even so, Louis's pro career started auspiciously. In his first fight, July 4, 1934, he knocked out his man, Jack Kracken, in one round and won a purse of fifty dollars. He fought steadily after that, knocking out ten men and taking decisions over two more. His opponents, all white, were men of considerable experience, and sports experts began to notice the man who was now called the Brown Bomber.

By the time of his first major fight, against the giant Italian, Primo Carnera, Joe's feet were on the glory trail. Carnera stood six-feet-six and weighed nearly 300 pounds. He had been built up by an unprecedented ballyhoo and many of his fights were acknowledged to be "setups," and many others were suspected of being fixed. Yet he had knocked out Jack Sharkey to win the heavyweight title in 1933, and he had defended successfully against the rugged Paulino Uzcudun and the aging but clever Tommy Loughran before losing the crown to Max Baer. But on that night in 1935, Carnera, the Man Mountain, as the sports writers called him, was no match for the twenty-one-year-old Louis. Joe was master of the situation from the first round on, pouring in a steady drumfire of rights and lefts that reduced the huge Carnera to a staggering hulk. In the sixth round, after the third knockdown, the big man was actually out on his feet and referee Arthur Donovan stepped in and stopped it.

Then came Louis's battle with Max Baer in the fall of 1935. Baer had been heavyweight champion for a year, having won by knocking out Carnera, but the clowning Californian had bowed that summer to Jimmy Braddock and had lost the crown. Baer was a magnificent boxer, but he was a carefree soul who did not believe in training very diligently. Nevertheless, Baer was backed heavily by his supporters who thought that his strong right hand would be too much for young Louis. Baer did manage a few blows on Louis's jaw, but Joe waded in relentlessly. In the third, he began nailing Baer with hard rights and lefts. Baer rocked and fell. He got up and fell again under a second shower of blows. He was dragged back to his corner, but as the fourth round began, Joe's right flashed and Baer was out for good.

After the Baer fight, taxicabs could not move in Harlem for the crowds of people in the streets. Louis had lifted the hearts of Afro-Americans as they seldom had been lifted in the century. And many a young black boy, listening on radio, took heart that some day he could become a fighter and a hero to his people as Joe Louis was.

Louis continued to win. He fought every three months or so, knocking out the supposedly indestructible Basque, Uzcudun, outpointing a running Bob Pastor, knocking out ex-champion Jack Sharkey. His string of undefeated bouts came to an end, of course, in the 1936 fight with Max Schmeling, but it was only a slight detour. The following year he knocked out champion James J. Braddock to win the heavyweight crown—the first black to do so since Jack Johnson—and, as we have seen, came back to destroy Schmeling in their celebrated return match.

Joe Louis held the crown for eleven years and though serving in the Army during World War II, twice defended his title—against Buddy Baer

Jersey Joe Walcott loses the heavyweight championship to Ezzard Charles, Chicago, 1949

and Abe Simon—for no purse. He donated more than $140,000 to service relief funds.

(While Louis was away, there were some half-hearted efforts to have him replaced as heavyweight champion, one Broadway wiseacre group going to the extent of organizing a White Hope tournament to find a white man to fight Louis after the war. At the announcement of that particular project, the White Hopes were assembled at Jack Dempsey's Restaurant to be introduced to the press. They lined up in boxing togs, about a dozen of them, and fourth from the left was a huge black man from Harlem. Jack Dempsey, who was hosting the introductions, came over to Red Smith, the sports writer, and said: "What do you think, Red?" Smith said, "Looks okay, champ, but how about that big one there?" Dempsey said, "Hey, you got a good eye, Red. He's the best White Hope of them all.")

Louis came out of the Army in 1946, and continued to meet all comers. In all, he defended the title twenty-five times, by far the record in boxing annals. He denied no challenger an opportunity, and if they put up a good fight the first time, as Billy Conn and Joe Walcott did, he gladly gave them a second chance. In no return match in his career, though, did Joe fail to improve on his first showing. If the challenger went the distance and lost the decision the first time, he was knocked out convincingly the second. When he gave up the title in 1949, and announced his retirement, Louis had an astonishing record: sixty-two fights, fifty-two knockout victories, nine triumphs by decision, one defeat.

By now, mainly because of Louis's exemplary conduct, not only as a fighter, but as an American (sportswriter Jimmy Cannon's line—"He is a credit to his race—the human race"—became part of the language), black fighters had broken through with unprecedented success. When an elimination tournament was held to fill the title vacancy left by Joe's retirement, the final match was resolved by two blacks, Ezzard Charles and Joe Walcott (called Jersey Joe Walcott to distinguish him from the early welterweight champion). Charles won by decision, and it was probably significant that he told reporters after the fight, "Look, I'm no Joe Louis and I know it."

Charles defended the crown listlessly against a few opponents of little stature, and then in 1950, Louis was convinced to come out of retirement to give boxing a shot in the arm. At the age of thirty-six, Louis was only a shadow of the Brown Bomber of old. Charles pounded him into a bleeding, helpless hulk and won a one-sided decision.

Charles held the title for only one more year when Joe Walcott beat him in Pittsburgh, Pennsylvania, and repeated the feat in the return match in Philadelphia. Walcott surrendered the title to the first white man to hold it since 1937, when Rocky Marciano knocked him out in 1952. Earlier, on his climb to fame, Marciano had knocked out poor old Louis in the last match of the Bomber's fistic career.

Marciano retired undefeated, and Floyd Patterson, another black who had a record of juvenile delinquency but had overcome that handicap, became champion by knocking out the venerable Archie Moore, who had been light heavyweight title holder, off and on, for a decade. Patterson gave up the crown to Ingemar Johansson of Sweden in 1959, and then decisively won it back by flattening the Swede in six rounds. He thus became the first heavyweight ever to regain the highest honor of the division.

Patterson lost the title in astonishing fashion in 1962, when Sonny Liston, a huge bear of a man, disposed of him in less than one minute of the first round. And when they met again in the summer of the following year, Liston again put Floyd Patterson away in the first few minutes of the opening round.

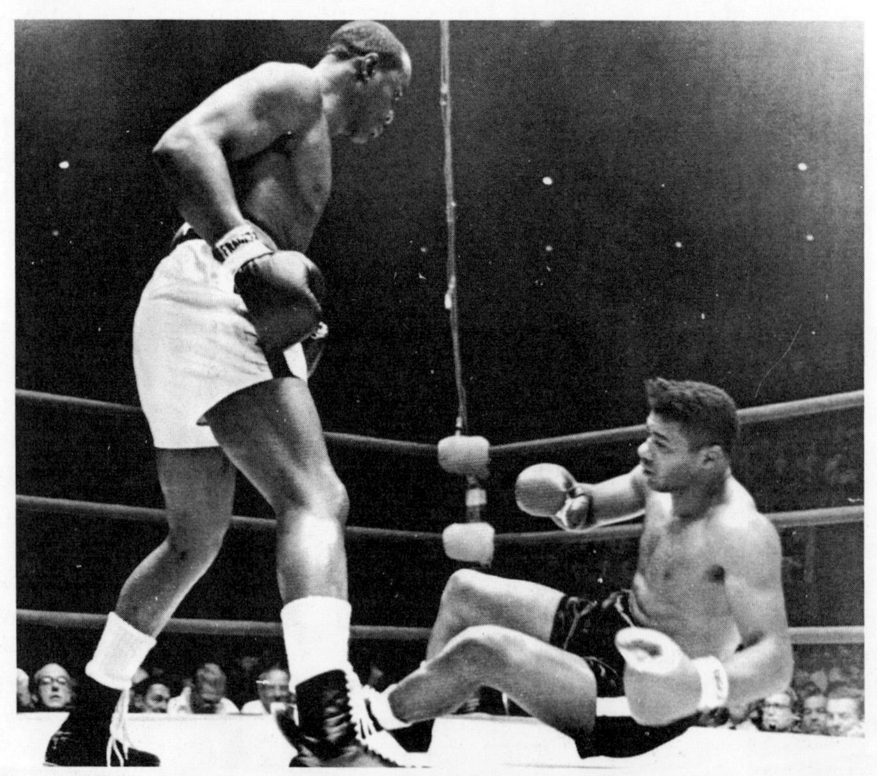

July, 1963 . . . Floyd Patterson is knocked down in the first round by world heavyweight champ Sonny Liston

"Hammerin' Henry" Armstrong, the only man to hold three titles simultaneously

The irrepressible and devastating Muhammad Ali burst on the fight scene in 1964. Ali, who had been known as Cassius Clay, had been an Olympic boxer for the U.S. in 1960, and emerged champion of the world light heavyweights at the age of eighteen. He was among other black fighters who won Olympic honors and turned professional, including Floyd Patterson (1952), Joe Frazier (1964), and George Foreman (1968). When Clay turned pro, he turned into a fullblown heavyweight—and never lost a fight. After demolishing Liston twice (seven rounds, one round), and Patterson with ease, the effusive Clay ("I Am the Greatest") blasted his way past all contenders. He defended ten times in two years until in 1967, when he became Muhammad Ali, and ran into difficulties, which will be related later.

Meanwhile, other black ace boxers were bursting into the spotlight on the heels of Joe Louis's phenomenal breakthrough. Henry Armstrong, a dynamic, tireless fighter from the West Coast, achieved one of the most remarkable feats in boxing history: he won three world titles in as many divisions within one year.

Hammerin' Henry, as the sports writers called him almost immediately, fought twenty-seven times in 1937, and in one of those bouts defeated Petey Sarron for the featherweight title (126-pound limit). In a few months Armstrong passed his division and challenged the welterweight (147 pounds) champion, Barney Ross, a fine boxer with a respectable wallop. Armstrong poured in a devastating fusillade of rights and lefts, boring in and shifting from body to face in a way that left the champion bewildered. Then, having won the feather and welter titles, Armstrong dropped down in weight to challenge Lou Ambers for the lightweight title (135 pounds). Ambers was a game foe, and the fight went a full fifteen rounds. But Armstrong carried the battle all the way through and got a convincing nod, thus becoming the only man to hold three titles at the same time.

Another renowned black who followed in Louis's wake was John Henry Lewis, who took over the light heavyweight crown by decisioning Bob Olin, who, in turn, had won it from the legendary Maxie Rosenbloom. Lewis, who was related distantly to the old champion, Tom Molyneux, abandoned the light heavy crown to become a heavyweight. John Henry had the misfortune to fight Joe Louis. He spotted the Bomber twenty pounds and went down in less than a minute of the first round.

Archie Moore, who took over the light heavy title fourteen years later to become the third black to wear the crown, held it through 1960. But he, too, ventured into the heavyweight ranks to be knocked out by Floyd Patterson. Moore by that time was of undetermined age (possibly forty-seven) and had been fighting for purses since before Floyd was born.

As America pulled out of World War II—which in some ways helped break down areas of discrimination and bigotry toward blacks—hundreds of others streamed into the professional boxing ranks. Less than five years after the war, four of the eight world championships were held by black fighters. Besides Joe Louis, these were Ray Robinson (welterweight), Ike Williams (lightweight) and Sandy Saddler (featherweight). Earlier, Beau Jack (real name Sidney Walker) and Bob Montgomery had held the lightweight crown, and for some time Chalky Wright had been recognized

Popular lightweight,
"Beau Jack"

as that title holder outside of New York. Jackie Wilson was in the same category, in the featherweight division.

Aside from Sugar Ray, who was to hold sway as an important boxing figure for a dozen years, probably the bustling Beau Jack was the most colorful. A golf caddy from Augusta, Georgia, the Beau fought six times in Madison Square Garden in 1943, grossing hundreds of thousands of dollars for his backers. Finally, Jack won the lightweight crown by beating Bob Montgomery. Then Montgomery won the next meeting, Jack the second and Montgomery the third. Ike Williams of Trenton, New Jersey, burst onto the scene now. He was recognized as the National Boxing Association title holder and when he beat Montgomery in 1947, became the undisputed world lightweight champion.

A sad footnote to this and earlier eras of boxing is the latter-day misfortune which often befalls champions, both black and white. Sports writer Al Laney, in 1944, found the very able and clever Sam Langford alone, blind and penniless in a dingy hall bedroom in Harlem. Langford had been a legendary fighter between 1902 and 1923, winning one hundred and fifty of two hundred and fifty bouts. Beau Jack, who drew hundreds of thousands of dollars to the arenas in his time, was discovered shining shoes in a Miami Beach hotel not many years ago. Countless similar tragedies have befallen lesser-known pugilists.

Light heavyweight Archie Moore

Sugar Ray Robinson, boxing's "superstar"

Sugar Ray Robinson was something else. He was a super-star in the mold of Louis and Jackie Robinson. One historian has called him "the greatest all-round fighter the ring has seen in our era, pound for pound, a whole career considered." Almost every major sports writer in the country has echoed these words.

Born in Detroit, Michigan, in 1920, Robinson grew up in the slum there known as Paradise Valley, in the worst years of the great depression. His real name was Walker Smith, Jr., and he was fourteen years old the year Joe Louis turned professional. From then on, Louis was the boy's idol, and as he practiced his fighting stance in front of the mirror, he dreamed of the time he would follow Louis into the ring. He had, in fact, seen Joe Barrow, as Louis was known then, when he fought in the amateurs. And one night—oh, glorious memory—Joe Barrow let young Smitty carry his bag.

Little Walker Smith's parents were divorced when he was seven. His mother went on relief. The neighborhood was tough and the teen-age gangs tougher, but the youngster was restrained from juvenile delinquency by an understanding mother and by a love for sports. Later, when the family moved to New York's Harlem, Junior, as his family called him, began boxing in Police Athletic League competition. At fifteen, he had the footwork of a professional and the punch of a fighter twice his age. He soon was fighting amateur bouts arranged by a man named George Gain-

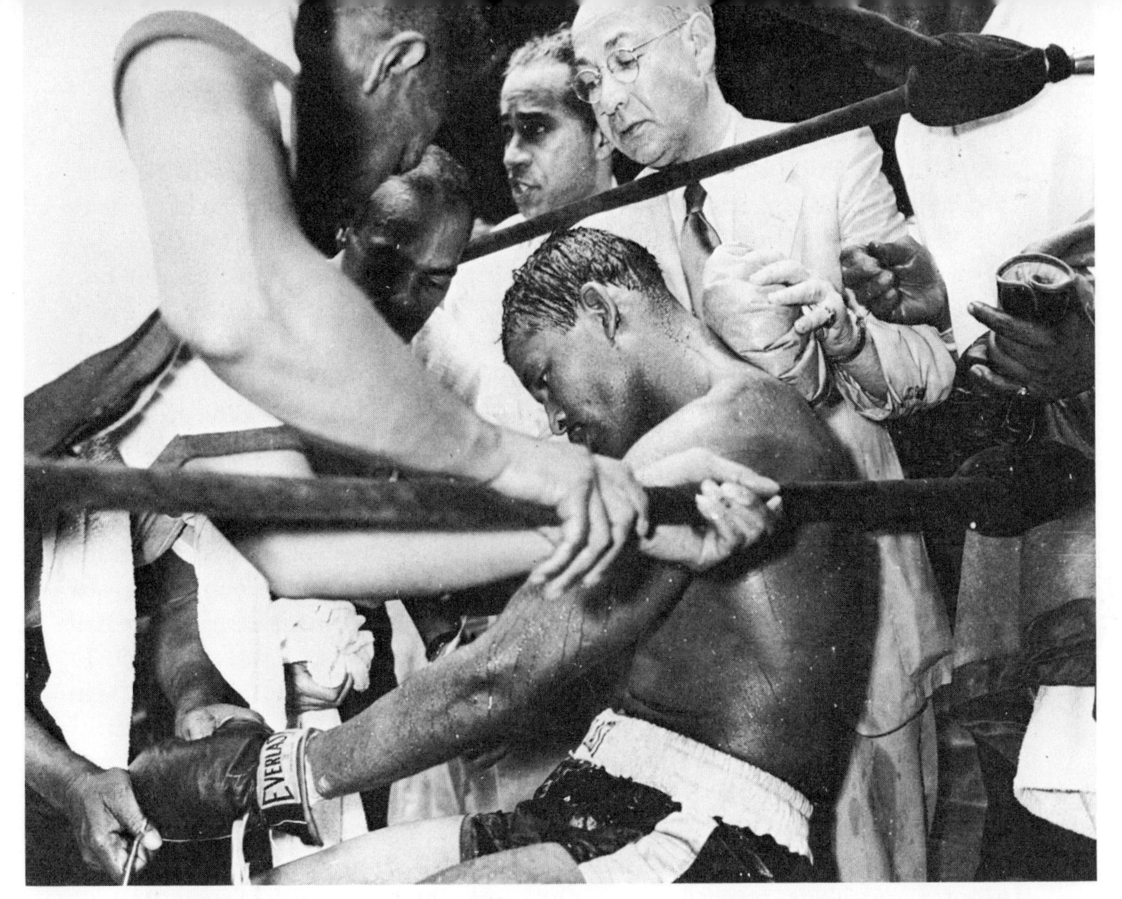

Defeat... Sugar Ray, unable to begin the fourteenth round of his bout with Joey Maxim, June 25, 1952

ford, who worked with neighborhood boys. In one of the Amateur Athletic Union fights, Junior filled in for a boy who did not show up. He had to borrow an A.A.U. card from a young fighter named Raymond Robinson. He won by a knockout and thereafter fought under the name Ray Robinson. When a sports writer one day said to Gainford, "That's a sweet boy you have there, George," Gainford smiled and said, "Sweet as sugar." And that name stuck too.

By 1940, when he was just twenty, Robinson turned professional after having won every one of his one hundred and twenty-five amateur matches. Sixty-nine were by knockouts and of those, forty-four came in the first round. A year after turning pro (fourteen victories in fourteen fights, twelve by K.O.), Robinson was a main event fighter. He moved up in class almost immediately. In 1941, he defeated the lightweight champion, Sammy Angot, in a non-title bout. He tried to get a fight with Fritzie Zivic, the welterweight king, but before a match could be arranged, Zivic lost the crown to Red Cochrane.

Zivic and Robinson met anyway later that year, Robinson winning a close decision, and in January, 1942, in a rematch, Ray knocked the capable Zivic, one of six fighting brothers, out cold in ten rounds. But Cochrane, the champion, joined the Navy and thus froze the championship and kept it out of Robinson's hands for the duration of the war.

But Sugar Ray now was an outstanding box office attraction and saw a great deal of action during the war. He took on a powerful Bronx puncher named Jake LaMotta in 1942, won a close decision and started what was to be a series of thrilling matches. In Detroit, at the beginning of 1943, LaMotta, a toe-to-toe battler, outrushed Robinson and would not permit him to make use of his classic boxing skills. The fight was a thriller in every way, and the crowd that jammed Detroit's Olympia Arena remained standing and emitted deafening roars throughout. In the sixth, LaMotta drove in close, worked a right to the body and a left hook to the jaw. Robinson went hurtling through the ropes and lay on the ring apron, barely able to get to his feet. He was saved by the bell.

But Robinson surged back and slugged toe-to-toe with the rugged LaMotta until the final bell. He could hardly be ashamed of the score handed down by the referee: five rounds, LaMotta; four rounds, Robinson; one even. But it did mark the end of Ray's remarkable winning streak that had reached a total of forty professional fights (thirty-two of them by knockout). And Ray could have said, but did not, that he was giving away fifteen pounds to the burly LaMotta.

Robinson was drafted almost immediately after the fight, but the Army allowed him a seven-day furlough, during which he fought LaMotta again in the same Detroit ring. The fight was another sizzler, but this time Ray managed to maneuver some boxing room, and though he was tagged by LaMotta and went down for an eight count in the seventh, Sugar Ray recovered quickly. He boxed smartly for the remaining three rounds and won the decision.

As a private first class in the U.S. Army, Robinson was disqualified for overseas duty because of a punctured eardrum. He was also permitted time off to participate in eight professional fights during his tour of duty and won them all. He later fought LaMotta on three other occasions and each was a hair-raising battle. Sugar Ray won all three. And after being uncrowned king of the welterweights for so long, he got a chance to make it official by whipping tough Tommy Bell in a hard-fought fifteen-round fight.

As champion of the welterweights, Robinson fought often, but usually he was matched in the heavier middleweight division. His record was remarkable. His old foe, Jake LaMotta, had won the title by beating Marcel Cerdan, a most able French boxer. Robinson was recognized by the State of Pennsylvania as middleweight title holder. So Robinson and LaMotta went at it again in February, 1951, in Chicago Stadium, with the world of television at ringside.

It was another classic bout. LaMotta had an early lead and, in fact, staggered Robinson with a crushing hook that drew blood in the fifth round. But in the seventh, with Robinson recovered, LaMotta appeared to slow down a trifle, and Robinson's skillful blows found their mark. Sugar Ray wore down LaMotta in the succeeding rounds and ended it in the thirteenth.

Then came a series of middleweight championship bouts that left fans bewildered. Robinson, now universally recognized as title holder, lost to Randy Turpin of England, and then thrashed him soundly in a return match to regain the crown. Robinson lost to Bobo Olsen next, and again regained the title in a return match. Gene Fullmer beat him, then Robinson took the crown back again. Carmen Basilio, the same. Finally, in 1959, Gene Fullmer again was recognized by the N.B.A., but Robinson held the New York title until Paul Pender came in.

Perhaps the weirdest fight of the century was waged in New York's Yankee Stadium in 1952, and Robinson was very much involved. The bout was for the light heavyweight championship of the world, Joey Maxim, title holder, 173 pounds. Robinson, still the middleweight king, came in at 157½. It was the hottest June 25 in New York history, and by fight time the temperature under the lights read 104 degrees. It was that brutal heat, not Joey Maxim, which conquered Sugar Ray that night.

Robinson was superb. Though thirty-one years old, he led the fighting from the start. Round after round he dominated his heavier opponent. His speed of foot and hand flashed in the night and kept his opponent off balance. Maxim clinched a good deal, but he was not able to land a substantial blow on the elusive Sugar Ray.

Robinson, despite the furnace-like heat, made all the fight. He outpunched and out-boxed the plodding champion and in the process exhausted himself. By the end of the tenth round, incidentally, the heat was so punishing that Ruby Goldstein, the referee, collapsed from heat prostration and had to be helped from the ring. He was replaced by Ray Miller, the first substitute referee ever in a title bout.

Three rounds later, after the thirteenth, the heartbreak came for Sugar Ray. He could not answer the bell for the fourteenth and Maxim was declared the winner and still champion. Robinson's own ambition and resourcefulness defeated him. He had played Maxim as though he were a violin, plinking him time and again, walloping him on occasion. The score card showed Robinson in front ten rounds to three when the bout abruptly ended. If he had only been able to stay on his feet for three more rounds of three minutes each, Sugar Ray would have been home free with his third championship (welterweight, middleweight, light heavyweight). Robinson was philosophical. "I wasn't beaten by Maxim," he said. "It was God's will that I finish that way."

He retired soon after that fight—but not for long. He continued to excite crowds with his dazzling ring mastery until he was well into his forties. There were few who denied him the right. Sports writer Red Smith, for one, would not protest. He called Robinson a fellow to be remembered. "Robinson skipping rope to music, all poetry and rhythm. Robinson punching the face off LaMotta. Robinson, wounded and desperate with pride, slugging tough Randy Turpin clear out of the middleweight division. If

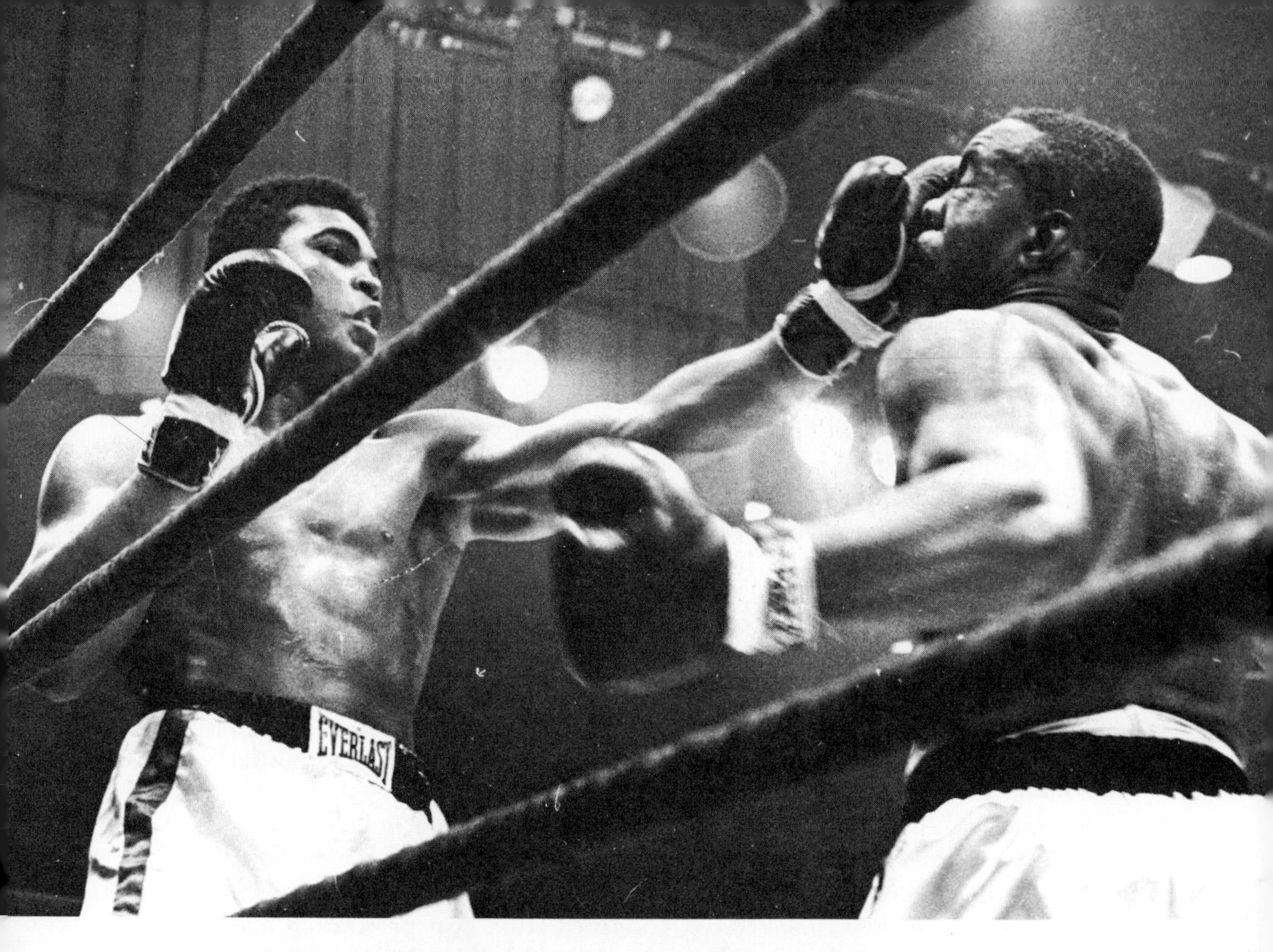

Ray wants another payday in the ring, he is entitled to it. If he prefers to take his rest, he earned it. In either event, he will have left us some memories."

There was a good deal of similarity in the classic moves of Sugar Ray Robinson and the style of Cassius Clay, who became Muhammad Ali. Clay-Ali has never been beaten in the ring, amateur or professional. In fact, like the legendary Jack Johnson, he is unmarked and unscarred. "I didn't go to the body," he said after one fight, "because I didn't want to get hit in the face. Body punchers get bruised, cut and swelled up. I like to be able to dress up the next day."

He was born in Louisville, Kentucky, on January 17, 1942, son of Cassius Marcellus Clay, Sr., a sign-painter, and Odessa Clay, a plump, gracious woman who insists that her elder son never was in a minute's trouble in his whole life. There is another son, who at birth was named Rudolph Arnett Clay. His brother later changed the name to Rudolph Valentino Clay. At twelve, young Cassius Clay began working out in the city's Columbia Gym at the prodding of an Irish cop named Joe Martin. At thirteen, he announced that he was going to win a medal for the United States in the Olympics. Five years later, he did exactly that, sweeping through his bouts seemingly with ease, and returning home with the gold medal, symbolic of the Olympic champion.

Sonny Liston takes a stiff left in his right eye from "The Greatest," Cassius Clay

He was unsophisticated then, everybody recalls, and it was predicted that his personality would be "a refreshing breeze in a becalmed sport." Backed by a Louisville syndicate of businessmen, he began fighting as a pro. He won nineteen straight, most of them by K.O., and he was matched with Sonny Liston, a hulking, scowling man who had won the heavyweight title by twice destroying Floyd Patterson, both times in the opening round. On the night of February 25, 1964, Ali scored a T.K.O. in the seventh round of their title fight—and he has not been defeated in the ring since.

He was a busy champion, though his prestige in the newspapers dipped badly. He had announced after the Liston fight that he had become a member of the Muslim faith, that he had bestowed upon himself a holy name because he had fulfilled the requirements of his faith and that he wished, thereafter, to be known as Muhammad Ali.

Most of the newspapermen made a joke of it. They advised him to cut out the nonesense and be a "credit to your race, the way Joe Louis was." The advice came thirty years too late, for in Joe Louis's time things were different. Louis had to prove himself to white sports writers to break a color line, just as Jackie Robinson had to prove himself ten years later. But the new Muhammad Ali was not to be budged. He did not listen.

Muhammad Ali stands over Sonny Liston after knocking him down during their 1965 re-match

Ali retained his title when he knocked out Liston during the first round of their May 25, 1965 bout

In the ring, a return match was arranged with Liston, but Boston boxing officials, where the fight was originally scheduled, refused sanction. They finally dragged the bout to Lewiston, Maine, where Liston was knocked cold in less than two minutes. Ali next took on Floyd Patterson and toyed with him for twelve rounds before knocking him out. He outpointed George Chuvalo in Toronto, Ontario, Canada; K.O.'d Henry Cooper and Brian London in London, England; won by a T.K.O. over Karl Mildenberger in Frankfurt, Germany, and beat three Americans, Cleveland Williams (T.K.O.), Ernie Terrell (decision) and Zora Folley (K.O.).

But a shadow fell over his career. It started on February 17, 1966, when Ali was reclassified 1-A in the selective service draft. He said he would not fight in Vietnam, and this drew the ire of veterans' groups and some politicians. The champion said his religion would not permit him to fight in a war.

In 1967, Muhammad Ali refused to be inducted into the Army. At the induction center in Houston, Texas, he refused to take the traditional one step forward, signifying joining of the service. He was rapidly convicted by a Houston jury of violating the draft law, sentenced to five years in prison and fined $10,000, the maximum punishment. His sentence was appealed by his attorneys and the champion remained free on $5,000 bond.

On the day he refused induction, officials of the New York State Athletic Commission—most powerful in the country—and officials of the World Boxing Association stripped Muhammad Ali Cassius Clay of his heavyweight crown.

Quickly, a new promotional group, Sports Action, Inc., organized an eight-man tournament to provide a successor. It was somewhat ironic that Jimmy Ellis, a black sparring partner of the champion, rapidly advanced to the final bout by disposing of Leotis Martin and Oscar Bonavena of Argentina. The other fighter was Thad Spencer, another black, who had beaten Floyd Patterson and Jerry Quarry of Los Angeles.

Many blacks were incensed at the stripping of Ali's title, insisting it was racial in origin. They said that a white Quaker of pacifist belief would not be sentenced to jail and they wondered aloud why a Muslim athlete drew such stiff punishment. One group of black amateur athletes organized informally and threatened to boycott the Olympic Games, giving the stripping of Ali's title as a partial reason.

CHAPTER IV

In the Beginning

Though it may come as a surprise to modern fans, Afro-American participation in baseball goes back to the 1860s. One Bud Fowler was the first black to play on an otherwise all-white team, starring at second base for the New Castle club of western Pennsylvania. And contrary to belief, Jackie Robinson was not the first black major leaguer. The pioneer big leaguer of a different color was Moses Fleetwood Walker, a college-educated player (Oberlin College in Ohio), who caught for the American Association's Toledo Club (1884), when that league was ranked as a major. He later was joined by his brother, Welday Wilberforce Walker, an outfielder. William Higgins, a second baseman, also made the big league, and others were on the way up from the white minors until the white backlash that followed the War Between the States brought on a color line that stood unchallenged for more than sixty years.

Afro-Americans probably started playing baseball while they still were slaves. The game had become popular long before the Civil War, for it was invented—or adapted from the British game of cricket—in 1845, by a bewhiskered surveyor named Alexander J. Cartwright. He is recognized as the founder by baseball's Hall of Fame in Cooperstown, New York, much to the chagrin of supporters of Abner Doubleday, who, legend had it, invented baseball in 1839.

In any event, the first college game was held in 1859, between Williams and Amherst. Big league baseball began in 1876, with the formation of the National League. But long before either of those dates, baseball in some form was being played by blacks in country towns below the Mason-Dixon line. When freedom was won, blacks drifted north, taking their baseball talents with them.

Satchel Paige, one of the first, and one of the greats

They must have been considerable, for despite high feelings against them, by 1880 twenty blacks were on minor league rosters as well as the sprinkling of big leaguers mentioned earlier. But in the years that followed, a hatred of blacks grew, fanned by Southern politicians, and the black players were done for.

One explosive incident occurred when the Chicago White Stockings, as they were known then, came to Toledo to play the Mudhens. The Walker brothers were in the lineup. Cap Anson, the Chicago manager and first baseman (and later a baseball immortal), stalked off the field when he saw the two blacks in uniform, and took his team with him. There was a large crowd in the stands. Charlie Morton, Toledo's manager, promised to fire the Walkers the next morning. The game was played.

Anson was not finished with the issue. He started a one-man crusade to rid the game of all but whites. He blocked the New York Giants from signing up a fine pitcher, George Stovy, who had struck out fifteen batters in an Eastern League game. Anson went to meetings of major and minor leagues and demanded adoption of a rule that would require owners to fire blacks on their rosters and never again to contract them. Twenty-five players lost their jobs and spent the remainder of their careers playing segregated ball.

One player thus shunted into obscurity was a fine second baseman for the Buffalo team. His name was Frank Grant, and he was known as the "Black Dunlap," an enormous compliment comparing him to Fred Dunlap, king of second basemen. Players made a habit of sliding into Grant, feet first, with their spikes flashing. He was injured so often that he finally wore wooden leg splints to protect his legs. But the opposing players sharpened their spikes with files and the first runner would hit Grant and split his wooden half cylinders. The second runner would hit flesh. Grant soon quit.

Barred from organized baseball, Afro-Americans formed their own teams. Waiters at a smart Long Island hotel formed the first one. To get games, they called themselves the New York Cuban Giants and passed as Cubans or Spaniards. To further the deception, the blacks put on an act and talked a gibberish on the field that was supposed to pass for Spanish.

One time this gave John McGraw, manager of the Giants and always hungry for victory, a smashing idea. He hired a fine black ballplayer, told him to keep his mouth shut and sent him to Cuba to come back as the new Giant star from Havana. The newspapermen caught on but said nothing. The player gave himself away and McGraw had to drop him.

On another occasion, McGraw found a slick second baseman named Charlie Grant playing on a sand lot in Hot Springs, Arkansas. McGraw turned Charlie Grant into a full-blooded Indian chief and named him Tokohoma. The ruse worked fine until Tokohoma went to Chicago for an exhibition game. Jubilant black fans jammed the stands, waving a banner: "Our Boy Charlie Grant!" McGraw, on orders from the league office, had to let Grant go the next day.

It is possible that some light-skinned blacks did "pass" into organized baseball at this period. Years later a story—completely without foundation—spread that Babe Ruth was black. But the vast, vast majority of Afro-Americans played ball in a world of their own.

Hundreds of independent black teams sprang up in the early part of the century. When the golden age of sports arrived in the United States in the Twenties, the two "big" leagues of black baseball, the Negro American and the Negro National, took firm root in the East and the West. They had a regular schedule, a World Series and often enthusiastic, huge crowds, many whites among them.

The caliber of play was exceptionally high. One game drew the attention of a Chicago sports writer, who commented in his paper: "The Negro game is faster on the bases than major league ball. It is almost as swift and spectacular in the field. It may lack the batting form of the white man's big league game, but the Newark shortstop, Willie Wells, is as good as a dozen men in that position in the majors today. It has pitchers who could fill places on half of the leading clubs of the top white leagues. The game was afire with speed. The bases were run with a swiftness and daring absent from the white man's game for years. They stretched singles into doubles, they went down to first so fast that no infield double play succeeded and the outfielders had whiplike arms and threw out base-runners daringly, as pitchers whipped bunts to second for force plays, a rarity in the white man's circuits."

Black fans always considered their stars as the equals, if not the superiors, of many whites whose names they read daily in the box scores. But those were the days of segregated churches, schools and theaters. Jesse Owens was making some waves in the track world and Joe Louis was becoming a national hero—yet organized baseball was closed.

Some of the players in those black leagues, whose feats never made the columns of white newspapers, became legends for young black boys—and for their fathers and grandfathers, too. One of these was a shortstop of the Twenties, John Henry Lloyd, who was such a tremendous talent at bat and in the field that one sports commentator said: "If you ask me the greatest player in organized baseball I'd say Babe Ruth, but if you mean in all baseball, the answer would be John Henry Lloyd."

Other stars included the colorful Rube Foster, who pitched black ball for twenty years and at one time served as pitching coach under John McGraw for the New York Giants in the era before World War I.

Amost everyone, black and white fan alike, has heard of Josh Gibson, the immortal black catcher. Once, the Homestead Grays, a fabled team of the league, played the Newark Eagles in a spring training game in Florida. The great Walter Johnson saw the game and said to Shirley Povich, the Washington sportswriter: "There is a catcher (Gibson) that any big league club would buy for $200,000. He can do everything. He hits the ball a mile. And he catches so easy he might just as well be in a rocking chair. Throws like a rifle. Even Bill Dickey (the best catcher in baseball at the time) isn't as good a catcher. Too bad this Gibson is a colored fellow."

Josh Gibson never made it into organized ball. Satchel Paige, the fabled pitcher, did finally—but only after he had spent thirty or thirty-five years in the black circuits. In those days, white major leaguers often played black teams in barnstorming post-season games, and Joe DiMaggio one time said that Paige was the toughest pitcher he ever faced. Paige had a series of post-season pitching duels with Dizzy Dean, when he was the greatest hurler in the game, and Paige invariably won.

Bill Yancey, who was a fine pitcher of the period, went on some of the barnstorming trips. Stars such as Lou Gehrig, Jimmy Foxx and Al Simmons furnished the opposition.

"But white baseball writers didn't cover our games, although we often drew 10,000 to 15,000 fans. No one scouted us. No one scouted Josh Gibson," Yancey said. "I've seen them all since the 1920's and Josh was the greatest right-hand hitter of all time. They say that Jimmy Foxx's homer to the last box in the third tier at Yankee Stadium was the longest blow ever made there. I was playing there against Josh's Homestead Grays and he lifted one two stories over the bull pen and out of the ball park."

Josh earned the top salary in the Negro leagues, $1,000 a month. He was still catching for the Homestead Grays in 1947, the year Jackie Robinson became a Dodger. "He was tickled to death the color line was broken," said Bill Yancey, "but he was a frustrated man, too old for the majors. Poor Josh let himself go. He got fat and quit in 1948. Two years later he died."

That $1,000-a-month was high pay, for most of the players earned less than $500, and often had to play three games in one day, ride all night on a rickety bus and often could not buy anything to eat because of the Jim Crow country through which they traveled.

One player, who was still playing black ball ten years after Robinson made the majors, described what the discrimination was like. It had not changed much from the day Cap Anson stalked off the field and refused to play against the Walker brothers.

"Down South, if you're playing in a white town, you don't eat. You can't get out of the bus. The secretary writes down all the stuff on a list and then hands it in the window, and then brings back the hamburgers and stuff. Wouldn't even let us come in out of the rain sometimes."

Despite conditions of this kind and scuffed-up infields and outfields where the weeds were knee-high, the Negro leagues produced scores of fine players who were never to see the inside of a first-class hotel.

They are names that are still remembered in many black homes today. They were all born a generation too early, for surely they would have broken into major league box scores just as today's black players are doing.

The list of Afro-American greats is long, but it would include Biz Mackey and Clarence Williams as catchers, Richard Redding, David Brown, William Foster, Stringbean Williams, Frank Wickware, Bullet Rogan, John Donaldson and, of course, Paige, and Rube Foster on the pitching staff. Foster not only was an outstanding pitcher but he was tireless in his early efforts to bring organization to black ball.

Star pitcher Satchel Paige finally made the Cleveland Indians

Other memorable names were Ben Taylor, Leroy Grant, Sam Hughes, Jud Wilson, Homerun Johnson, Andrew Jackson, Oscar Charleston, Peter Hill, Chester Brooks and Fats Jenkins. The all-star squad could also include Frank Warfield, Bingo Demoss, Henry Blackman, Bill Monroe, Eddie Douglass, Spotswood Poles, Jap Payne, Peter Washington and Oliver Marcelle.

As the years passed and baseball's ban on Afro-Americans persisted, voices were raised in protest. This was particularly true in the socially conscious Thirties when pressure began forcing other sports to open their doors to blacks. Many sports writers joined the crusade, including the great Heywood Broun and Jimmy Powers of the *New York Daily News.* Baseball turned a deaf ear, arguing that white players would revolt, that spring training in the South would be disrupted because of housing difficulties for blacks, and that—besides—blacks wanted to play in their own league. The voices of protest against discrimination grew louder—but baseball owners refused to listen.

The Thirties ran into World War II and millions of Afro-Americans went into the armed forces. War was a great leveler, and many Southerners who had never even accepted blacks as human beings before, learned to know them and live with them. The United States was a different country by the end of the Second World War.

Throughout the war, the drive to get blacks into big league competition had not slackened. The black press and many whites of good will put the question bluntly to the high lords of baseball: "Why?"

At the time there was a black second lieutenant in command of an all-black tank battalion, stationed at Camp Hood, near Waco, Texas. His name was Jackie Robinson. He had been a football, baseball and basketball star at the University of California at Los Angeles and his brother, Mack, had been on the 1936 Olympic team. Jackie Robinson was separated from service late in 1944, and the following spring, he signed to play ball with the Kansas City Monarchs of the National Negro League.

Wendell Smith, a sportswriter for the black *Pittsburgh Press,* had been pounding away at baseball's color line. He had succeeded, in 1945, in getting the Boston Red Sox to agree to "look over" a few black players. Smith, having covered Robinson's Negro League games, asked him to go along for the tryout, as well as two other League players, Sam Jethroe and Marvin Williams. The three blacks had their workout at Fenway Park in Boston, but though officials told them they would be notified if wanted, the trio never heard from the club again.

There was another tryout fizzle that spring. Smith and Joe Bostic of the *Peoples' Voice,* in New York City, managed to get two veteran black players into Brooklyn Dodger uniforms. They were Terris McDuffie and Dave Thomas. The Brooklyn decision was that they were too old to start in as major league rookies.

Robinson scores . . . and helps the Montreal Royals defeat the Jersey City Giants, April 4, 1946

Despite the absence of Afro-Americans on big league diamonds for sixty-five years, baseball spokesmen still insisted that there was no color line. Judge Kenesaw Mountain Landis, the Commissioner of Baseball, repeatedly said that no "formal or informal understanding, unwritten, subterranean or sub-anything" against the hiring of blacks existed. He said, "The hiring of blacks is up to club owners."

Then one day in Chicago, where Jackie Robinson's club was playing, he was approached by Clyde Sukeforth, a coach for the Brooklyn Dodgers. He wanted to know if Robinson would go to New York to see Branch Rickey. He did not know why Rickey wanted to see Jackie. Robinson had heard there was a third Negro League being organized with a Brooklyn club in it. Perhaps that was the reason.

"All right," said Jackie Robinson, "I'll go." He took a train that night, heading East to Brooklyn, U.S.A.

He did not know it, but a revolution was about to take pace. And he was to be its central figure.

Jackie Robinson, 1946

Dodgers
1946
ECTRICITY more for your m
HE
STRIKES
BALLS
OUTS
BATTING ORDER
UMPIRES
PLATE
BASES
ABE STARK
Burma-Shav
WATCH FOR
DANNY KAYE
VIRGINIA MAYO

CHAPTER V

The Baseball Revolution

If Jackie Robinson was the symbol of the revolution in baseball, Branch Rickey was its architect. Rickey, sixty-four years old, had been a driving force in the baseball business all his life. Three years earlier he had taken over as president and general manager of the Brooklyn Dodgers and had begun rebuilding a team that had won only one pennant (1941) in more than twenty years. He quietly began, as part of his rebuilding efforts, checking out black prospects, among them Jackie Robinson. Rickey knew how momentous the move would be, for although he had the backing of his board of directors in Brooklyn, the rest of the baseball club owners was unanimously against it. Rickey once revealed that at a major league joint meeting in 1945, he had attempted to raise the question. Of the fifteen clubs represented, fourteen adopted a resolution opposing blacks in big league ball.

Rickey's scouting efforts were secret. Even the scouts he sent out to look over black players did not know why they were doing it. Rickey disguised his intentions from all but his own family. As the reports came in, one name popped up time and again. The name was Jackie Robinson of the Kansas City Monarchs. He filled all the requirements Rickey thought necessary for breaking the color line.

The historic meeting between Rickey and Robinson took place on August 28, 1945. Jackie was wary as he entered. He recalls wondering why the bushy-browed Rickey immediately launched into a series of personal questions. Did he have a girl? Did he get along well with his white teammates and coaches at U.C.L.A.? Why was he discharged from the Army? Robinson stammered as he answered: "Yes, Yes, an old football ankle injury."

Signing with Montreal . . . Jackie Robinson joins the Royals as Branch Rickey, Hector Racine and J. Romeo Gauvreau look on

Then Rickey dropped the bomb: "Jackie, you were brought here to play for the Brooklyn organization. Perhaps in Montreal to start with. Later on—if you can make it—you'll have a chance with the Dodgers."

Robinson's head was swimming. He wondered to himself, remembering the tryout fiasco with the Red Sox, if this were just another pipe dream that would build his hopes only to burst at the last minute. Robinson could only nod.

"But I want you to understand, young man," Rickey thundered, "this is going to take more than just playing. I wish it meant only hits, runs and errors—things you can see in a box score—"

Robinson found his voice: "Mr. Rickey, when the chips are down, isn't what they put in the box score what really counts?"

"That's all that ought to count, but isn't," said Rickey. "Maybe one day it *will* be all that counts. But right now you have to be bigger, even more courageous than that. You'll be insulted, players will try to spike you, throw at your head—"

"Mr. Rickey," Jackie said, "they've been throwing at my head for a long time."

Rickey's voice rose. "Suppose I'm a player, and in the heat of an important ball game . . ." Rickey got up as if to charge at Robinson . . . "and we collide at second base and I get up and yell, 'You dirty, black, son of a—' What do you do?"

Robinson licked his lips and swallowed. In a quiet voice he said, "Mr. Rickey, do you want a ballplayer who's afraid to fight back?"

"I want a ballplayer with guts enough *not* to fight back," Rickey roared. "You got to do this job with base hits and stolen bases and fielding ground balls, Jackie. Nothing else!"

For three hours Rickey explained to the ballplayer what pitfalls and horrors he must expect. He posed as a prejudiced hotel clerk denying him a room, a sneering waiter not serving him, a biased sports writer twisting stories—even violent anti-black players spiking him and even punching him.

"What do you do when that man hauls off and belts you in the cheek?"

"Mr. Rickey," Jackie almost whispered, "I've got two cheeks. That it?"

Rickey breathed a sigh. He was satisfied with his man. That fall, shortly after the World Series, the next-to-last Series to be played without black participants, Rickey released the news that Robinson was to play for the Montreal Royals of the International League.

Robinson was home with his family in Pasadena when Rickey wired him to fly to Montreal and sign. His arrival was a turning point in the history and character of the game. It may even be said it was a turning point in the history of this country. Nothing comparable ever happened in another sport. Joe Louis and Jesse Owens were individual champions; Robinson was asked to make good and win the respect of teammates, coaches, writers and fans, many of them steeped in the dark tradition of bigotry.

Nowhere in the past was one man, hand-picked deliberately, sent out to face the forces of discrimination.

They came out of their holes with a vengeance when the story broke. Inside baseball, men began hammering at Rickey and Robinson both openly and behind their backs. The head of the minor leagues, a since-forgotten W. G. Bramham, called Rickey a "carpetbagger." The late Clark Griffith, who owned the Washington Senators then and rented his park for many Negro League games, became concerned with the rights of Negro League players. *The Sporting News,* baseball's quasi-official weekly, thought Jackie's baseball abilities might make him eligible "for a trial with a Class B farm club—if he were six years younger." Rogers Hornsby, a Hall of Fame great, snapped from Texas: "Ballplayers on the road live close together . . . it won't work." Even Bob Feller, who had pitched against Robinson in one exhibition game, felt qualified to remark: "Good field—no hit. Sucker for an inside pitch." Dixie Walker, from Birmingham, Alabama, who, the story goes, had to wait two years before he could admit to his old grandma that he played for the Yankees, said that he wouldn't worry "until he joined the Dodgers." The president of the Texas League said flatly: "I'm positive you'll never see any black players on any teams in the South." Happy Chandler, then Commissioner of Baseball, had no comment.

Many others had comments, though. "He will never make the grade . . . a 1,000-to-one shot," declared Jimmy Powers, sports editor of the *New York Daily News,* a tabloid with the largest circulation in the country. "The Negro player will be so uncomfortable, embarrassed and out of place that he will soon get out of his own accord," said a Durham, North Carolina, sports writer. Joe Williams, another eminent New York sports editor, dismissed the news by saying, "Blacks have been kept out of big league ball because they are, as a race, very poor ball players. The demands of the black often bulk larger than his capabilities." Stanley Frank, of the liberal *New York Post,* decided race riots would ensue when "Southern players brandish spikes with intent to cut and maim black infielders." There were other sportswriters and editorialists, of course—among them Red

Smith, Stanley Woodward, Shirley Povich, Jimmy Cannon, Grantland Rice—who applauded the move as an example of democracy in action.

All of the dissenters were wrong, but the early years *were* rough for Robinson. In spring training with Montreal in 1946, at Sanford, Florida, Jackie and his wife (he had married his U.C.L.A. sweetheart) ran into Jim Crow busses and had to room in black homes. Later, the Robinsons were compelled to leave Sanford; Jackie was ordered off a ball field by police; games were canceled because Florida towns would not stand for a black competing against whites. Some of the players resented Robinson at first, though not openly. There were no flare-ups. And though Clay Hopper, the Royals manager, was no great fan of Rickey's experiment ("You don't really think blacks are human beings, do you?" he once asked Rickey), he was fair. Robinson has often said that Hopper gave him every break.

That year Montreal opened in Jersey City, where opening day was always a municipal festival under Mayor Frank Hague. The way Hague ran things, city employees had to buy tickets for the opener but did not have to attend the game. But this was a day worth remembering. A black was playing his first League game in organized baseball. A crowd of 25,000 people was on hand.

That crowd included the present writer, just discharged from the Army and not yet on a newspaper baseball beat. With a friend who took half a day off from work, the writer took the Hudson Tubes to the Jersey City park. Years later I asked that friend if he remembered.

"Remember?" he said. "For all the days of my life. You have to put the time of that game in historic perspective. We were just coming out of the war and a lot of us thought that because of the kind of war it was, we were going into a new era. Robinson was one of the products. Robinson breaking the color line was part of the history of my time. Maybe that sounds like a heavy way to describe a ball game, but remember when it happened. Then it looked as if nothing was going to be impossible in the new world we'd made by winning the war. If the war hadn't happened, Jackie would have been in a machine shop or a Negro "Y" gym.

"And how did he respond to the pressure? It was like a fairy tale. I can still tell you everything he did. He hit a homer with two men on his second time up. He got three other hits, two by beating out bunts. He stole two bases, scored four runs and twice rattled the Jersey City pitcher into making scoring balks. The score was 14–1, Montreal. I'll never forget that ride home in the Tubes. Sheer exuberance. The war meant something, after all."

In 1946, Robinson won the International League batting championship with an average of .349. He led the League in fielding (at second base) with a .985 average and stole forty bases. Montreal was in front by fifteen games by August 1. In the Little World Series the Royals met the Louisville Colonels for the minor league championship. The games played in the Kentucky city were tense almost to the point of anguish. The club owners had put a quota on the number of black fans who could attend, and that intensified the underlying tension.

The Series was close, but Jackie emerged the hero in the final game. Montreal rooters swarmed on the field, cheering wildly, trying to get near him. He had to be protected from his admirers. Sports writer Sam Martin wrote: "It was probably the only day in American history that a black man ran from a white mob that had love on its mind insted of lynching."

Jackie's trials weren't over, though. The following year he came up to the Dodgers and was moved to a strange position, first base. Brooklyn won the pennant with ease. Robinson's performance was astonishingly good. He hit .297, led the League in stolen bases and sacrifice bunts, and his 175 hits assured everybody that he could handle big league pitching. But despite all this, Robinson had to listen to vicious insults. He had to keep reminding himself of Rickey's admonition: "Don't fight back."

Manager Ben Chapman of the Phillies unloaded a string of epithets when the season was only two weeks old. Once a Chicago Cub base runner kneed him in the groin. Ewell Blackwell, the Cincinnati pitcher, stopped pitching long enough to call him a long series of names. "Come on, throw the ball," was all Robinson permitted himself to say. The anonymous letters he received were vicious and ugly.

There was even an attempted strike by the St. Louis Cardinals. But Stanley Woodward, one of the great sports editors, found out about it, printed the story and Ford Frick, then president of the National League, moved in with force. He threatened the men who said they would strike with life suspension from the game. The uprising died aborning.

In that first year, Robinson was named Rookie of the Year by *The Sporting News,* the publication which had suggested that if he were white, he would only be good enough for Class B ball. The paper commented: "Robinson was rated and examined solely as a freshman player in the big leagues —on the basis of his hitting, his running, his defensive play, his team value. The sociological experiment that Robinson represented, the trail-blazing he did, the barriers he broke down, did not enter into the decision."

But it had to enter into everything Robinson touched. It was still too

1947 . . . Leo Durocher of Brooklyn greets Jackie Robinson

Catcher Roy Campanella, who made baseball's Hall of Fame in 1969

early for everybody to consider him just another good ballplayer. That was to come later when scores of other Afro-Americans came to the major leagues and when his teammates and the writers traveling with him stopped referring to him as the "*Negro* star." He was simply the Dodger second baseman, the position to which he was shifted after 1947. Accepted by his teammates, Robinson began discarding the "armor of humility" for which Branch Rickey had outfitted him. He argued on umpires' decisions, answered the shouts of the bench jockeys and took exception to high slides and beanballs. By 1949, he was a fiery, no-holds-barred competitor, and that was the way he remained for his ten years in the major leagues.

In 1949, the Dodgers won another pennant, with Robinson leading the league in hitting and being voted Most Valuable Player. Within two years he had zoomed from the player "who'll never make the majors" to the best performer in his league. Jackie quit after the 1956 season with a lifetime batting average of .311, and a history of being one of the most exciting players in the game. One of his fiery rivals, Leo Durocher, once said: "When it came to the key spot of winning or losing a ball game, Robinson was the one man I feared the most." Jackie dominated his time in the game.

Five years after his retirement, the required waiting time, he was elected to baseball's Hall of Fame, the first black to achieve this honor. It was a fitting tribute for Robinson, the ballplayer. But there is no Hall of Fame big enough to honor Robinson, the pioneer. His contribution to America was to pull us all closer together. He showed the way for hundreds of players of his color. He gave pride to millions of people.

Once, shortly after Jackie came into the league, this writer was covering a game at Brooklyn's old Ebbets Field. From the press box one could look out the back window and study the fans in the upper deck behind home plate. One scrutinizing that part of the crowd, much of it black, as it often was after Robinson broke the color line, could study the faces. There were old men and old women, young men with their girls, teen-agers and little kids. They ate their franks, drank their pop and whistled and cheered for the Dodgers. Then Jackie would knock down a liner or scramble from first to third in that pigeon-toed way he had. The faces would light up and take on a look of such undiluted bliss, of such bursting pride, that a stranger looking on might have imagined he was in church.

Another reporter came over and stood at the window. After a while he said: "They waited a long time for him." And they had: Sixty years, to be exact.

But despite Jackie Robinson's emergence as a star of the first magnitude, baseball owners seemed in no hurry to follow Branch Rickey's lead. The Brooklyn president had signed four other Afro-Americans—John Wright, Roy Partlow and Don Newcombe, pitchers, and a catcher who was to achieve greatness, Roy Campanella—and had sent them to the minor leagues. Rickey was trying to find an ally among owners in his battle for integration. All turned a deaf ear, except Bill Veeck, then president of the Cleveland Indians and a maverick ready to embrace any innovation to help the game.

Veeck signed Larry Doby, the first black in the American League, in July 1947. He had been born in Camden, South Carolina, had emigrated from the South in his boyhood to Paterson, New Jersey, and had become a

Larry Doby, the first black in the American League, a year after he signed with Cleveland

four-letter man with all-state and all-metropolitan honors at East Side High School. As an athletic hero, he had not experienced discrimination.

Then Doby signed on with the Newark Eagles in the Negro National League, and though the travel was rough and the food poor, he was young and enjoyed himself. After a Navy hitch, Doby rejoined the Eagles, was scouted by Veeck and became a big leaguer as an infielder. The following year the Indians won the pennant, Larry hitting .301. He had been switched to the outfield. He also acquired a roommate—he had never roomed with white players—the fabled Satchel Paige, who was a strong man in Cleveland's bullpen that season.

The St. Louis Browns then bought Henry Thompson and Willard Brown from the Kansas City Monarchs, but they played only a handful of games before being released. Later, Thompson had an eight-year career of some note with the New York Giants, getting into two World Series, but Willard Brown sank back into the Negro League.

The black players who did make it were very good indeed. They gave club owners much food for second thoughts. For not only were they interested in fresh talent, if they could find it, but they were not unaware of the black dollar which was piling into the box offices of clubs with black players.

In 1950, the New York Giants brought in Monte Irvin and Hank Thompson. Then the Braves (then in Boston, later in Milwaukee and still later in Atlanta) bought the speedy Sam Jethroe from Branch Rickey for $150,000, and Jethroe became a first-rate outfielder, base stealer and a six-time All-Star.

Gradually, other clubs got in the swim. There were, naturally, inept black players and some of the clubs got stuck. Some picked inept players on purpose so they could say, "See? We tried one and he didn't make it." But many of the pioneers became outstanding. The Cubs signed Ernie Banks, who made the All-Star team eight times. The Dodgers were winning the pennant with regularity with a lineup heavy with players of dark skin: Robinson, Campanella, Dan Bankhead, Don Newcombe, Jim Gilliam.

By 1951, integration was accepted as a way of life in baseball except in a few backward quarters. By 1959, black players were on every big league club with the Red Sox the last of the pre-expansion teams to succumb.

As the ranks of Afro-American players grew, they found a new acceptance—an acceptance based on their skills. The color of their skin did not matter. In the newspapers Robinson became "the Dodgers' star second baseman," not "the Dodgers' *Negro* star." Race-baiting as a form of bench jockeying slowly disappeared. In the beginning Robinson and Doby took a lot of ugly slurs based on supposed black characteristics (rivals brought watermelons and shoe shine kits into the dugout), but that too passed. Many white players tore into the race-baiters of their own clubs.

Soon, white and black players were playing cards together on the road, going to movies together and trading baseball talk in hotel lobbies. Dixie

The incredible Willie Mays

Walker, the unreconstructed rebel who at one time had asked to be traded when Jackie Robinson joined the Dodgers (Rickey accommodated him later), quietly pulled Robinson aside one day and lectured him on how to hit behind runners and avoid hitting into double plays. Once Robinson received a crank letter warning him he would be shot from the stands in Cincinnati. His teammates rallied around, even ribbing him about it. "Let's all wear Number 42 on our backs today," said Gene Hermanski. Jackie said: "O.K., and don't forget to paint your faces black and run pigeon-toed."

Whites were learning—as others had discovered on Ford Motor Company assembly lines, in Bethlehem Steel plants and in adjoining hospital beds in Army installations—that bigotry could not survive integration.

By the time the superb Willie Mays came to the big time in 1951, much of the bitterness had worn off, thanks to the efforts of the pioneers and the innate decency of most players and managers. Mays became a superstar and would have been so considered regardless of color. It is an interesting note that Mickey Mantle, the Yankees' explosive ace, came up the same year as Willie Mays. And though arguments raged across the country as to who was better, discussion leveled on performance at the ball park. The color question was never raised.

There are those who say that Mays is the most exciting player in the history of the game. Certainly he is no worse than third or fourth. One current historian has written: "Mays brings a hot passion to the field. He has contributed much more to baseball than his talent, his astonishing statistics, his home run feats, his great throw and catches, and his daring sprints on the base paths. None of us has ever seen a man with greater mercurial talent, a greater excitement quotient. He can do so much so well and so excitingly. Watch him on the sidelines before a ball game, tossing a ball back and forth with a teammate, and you see the incredible grace, the flowing strength, the swift and nimble hands. But more important is the latent explosion which colors everything he does. Mays lights up the sport."

Born in a suburb of Birmingham, Alabama, on May 6, 1931, Mays was playing catch with his father at the age of three. By the time he was ten, his natural baseball talent thrust him into sand lot games with boys four and five years older. By fourteen, he was pitching for a semi-pro steel mill team. In high school, he was a basketball and football star before he launched his baseball career with the Birmingham Barons, a black team.

Three years later Willie Mays was the New York Giants' center fielder, was chosen Rookie of the Year and played in the World Series. He was twenty years old. In the next eighteen years, he got into two more World Series, was chosen Most Valuable Player twice, won four home run titles, one batting title and was named to the National League All-Star team for thirteen consecutive years (1954-1966). He amassed a total of more home runs than anyone in the history of the game, save the mighty Babe Ruth. By 1968, Mays was the game's highest paid player, $125,000 a year.

Though Mays won honors as a superstar, there were scores of other Afro-Americans who were not far behind. In the twenty-one years A.J. (After Jackie), eleven blacks and one Latin-American were named the year's best rookies in the National League, one black and two Latin-Americans in the American League. The selections were good barometers of progress: Don Newcombe, Sam Jethroe, Mays, Joe Black, Jim Gilliam, Frank Robinson, Willie McCovey, Billy Williams, Richie Allen and Orlando Cepeda from Puerto Rico. The American League could boast only two blacks—Rod Carew and Tommy Agee—and two Latin-Americans—Luis Aparicio and Tony Oliva—over the same period. The preponderance of bright black talent which flocked to the National League, some people think, explains why this group has won fifteen of the last twenty All-Star games and nine of fourteen World Series.

Blacks or Latin-Americans have won fifteen batting crowns since 1949 and thirteen home run crowns. They have all but dominated selections for the annual All-Star games, held each summer between the best of each league.

It cannot be said that there is anything about black genes that makes for better ballplayers. That would not only be inverse bigotry, but utter nonsense. The answer is that Afro-Americans, after being sidelined for so long by our national pastime, received their chance. There will be more good ball players in a lot of a thousand black and white youths than in a lot of five hundred white youths alone. The Yankees of New York, among the last to hire a black or Latin-American player, found themselves plummeting from almost perennial champions of the world to dead last in their own league because their white talent pool dried up and they had ignored dark-skinned athletes for so long. To be sure, the Yankees had hired a few black players. Elston Howard, their fine catcher, for instance, played in nine World Series, and was named Most Valuable Player one year, and Al Downing, a lefty pitcher, got into a couple. But the fact remained that the Yankees had little taste for black players and suffered accordingly.

Howard, of course, became the first black man to coach in the American League in 1969. The Yankees assigned him to the first-base coaching job as a reward, probably, for his distinguished service, even though they had traded him off to the Red Sox late in his career. As coach he joined Jim Gilliam, Dodgers; Gene Baker, Pirates and Satchel Paige, Braves, all National Leaguers, who paced the black entrance to the coaching box. (Ernie Banks, Cubs, was still listed as "player-coach" in 1969.) The guessing was still wild on the first choice for first black big league manager. The favorite surmises were Maury Wills, Bill White and Howard. In earlier years it had been assumed that Roy Campanella would be the first, but he was crippled when his car skidded on ice and thereafter was confined to a wheel chair.

Despite Howard, however—and many observers thought he was a "token" gesture made by the Yankees—the club continued to languish in the second division in a period when other clubs were building. The Yankees seemed to have missed the boat.

On the other hand, the clubs which had scouted and developed and polished black and Latin players found themselves in commanding positions. The Red Sox of Boston, for instance, the last team in baseball to employ a black (Pumpsie Green in 1959), won their first pennant in 1967, when they lowered their color bars completely. With blacks George Scott, Elston Howard and Reggie Smith and Cuban José Tartabull and Puerto Rican José Santiago, the Red Sox won the pennant on the last day of the season.

But they ran into the Cardinals of St. Louis in the World Series. And the Cards had some dark-skinned aces of their own, including pitcher Bob Gibson, who won three games in the Series; the spectacularly speedy duo, Lou Brock and Curt Flood, all black; Orlando Cepeda, the big Puerto Rican first baseman, and Julian Javier, second baseman from the Dominican Republic. The Series was hard fought and went the full seven games. These were the men in the spotlight.

In the following World Series—Detroit vs. the Cardinals—Gibson struck out seventeen men in the opening game for a new record. Lou Brock was again outstanding, even though the Tigers won the Series in seven games.

Among pace setters for Afro-Americans in baseball over the years were Buck O'Neil, a one-time National Negro League great, who was named a

Baseball's modern superstar, Bob Gibson

coach with the Chicago Cubs in 1962. The Dodgers retained Jim Gilliam as their coach, starting in 1965. Though there have been no big league managers, there have been a number of minor league clubs managed by blacks, including Sam Bankhead, Chet Brewer, Nate Moreland, Marv Williams and Gene Baker. Emmett Ashford, an umpire in the Pacific Coast League, was promoted to the American League in 1966, to pioneer another field for blacks. He became instantly popular with his flamboyant gestures, and ballplayers said he was one of the best umpires in the league. Cleveland also hired a "front office" man, Louis Jones, once married to singer Lena Horne, in 1947.

Meanwhile, by Opening Day, 1968, the rosters of major league clubs bulged with black and Latin-American stars and journeymen. A heartening sign for America was that not one incident of a racial nature had marred play. At long last, the men who ran baseball in this country had decided, as Branch Rickey had long ago, that they wanted the best possible players, regardless of color. As a result, it often seems that there are no inept black players. If it seems that way, it is because there has been a thorough screening and only the cream of the black and Latin-American crop reaches the big time.

Lou Brock of the St. Louis Cardinals collides with Cincinnati Reds' catcher Johnny Bench

20

Over-all, of the five-hundred major leaguers at the start of the 1968 season, 187 were either black or Latin-American, a whopping percentage of 37.4. By 1969 the figure was even higher. When compared with the twelve per cent of the population that these groups comprise, the figure becomes all the more astonishing. In addition, of the 160 players who made up Opening Day lineups on the twenty clubs, aside from the pitchers, there were 73 of dark skin, a percentage of 45.6.

This figure of starting lineup players, the cream of the cream of American ballplayers, broke down to 49 Afro-Americans (30.3 per cent), eleven Cubans, five natives of the Dominican Republic, three Puerto Ricans, three Venezuelans, two Mexicans and a Panamanian.

They were warm, comforting numbers for those who believed in the future of American democracy.

Lou Brock in action against the Chicago Cubs

CHAPTER VI

Football for Love

American football grew out of English rugby which in turn grew out of English soccer or, as it was called, English football. It was only a game of kick-the-ball until a man named William Webb Ellis, playing for Rugby College in 1823, picked up the ball and ran with it. His opponents hurled him to the ground for his unsporting act, but it was a momentous act. It started the development of modern football.

As the game grew in the United States in the early nineteenth century, big Eastern colleges used it as an excuse for a free-for-all between the freshman and sophomore classes. One player would gingerly put a finger or toe to the ball, and that was the signal for various class members to set upon one another with deadly intent. The riot would go on until one class or another reached the "goal." At Harvard, football day was known as Bloody Monday.

Authorities were disturbed and abolished the sport, if that's what it was. It bounced up again, though, in various forms. Some colleges played the old-fashioned soccer game, called "Association" (the soccer name coming from a corruption of the abbreviation "assoc."). Other colleges played a form of rugby and still others played a combination of the two, usually with twenty-five men to a side.

Eventually, the colleges got together to set up uniform rules. The teams were reduced to fifteen players on a side, touchdowns and penalties were defined and an oval ball, instead of the round, black rubber one that had been in use, was introduced. Later, the teams were reduced to eleven men. The first intercollegiate game took place a hundred years ago between Princeton and Rutgers in 1869. Soon, Columbia, Yale, Michigan,

Cornell and Harvard also had teams, and the game was refined to reduce violence (such as punching a rival in the nose with clenched fist). A rule was brought in requiring a team to advance the ball ten yards in four downs or less, or give up the ball to the other side. Another rule countenanced the straight-arm for the runner and protective body blocking by his teammates. Thus, at the turn of the century, American football, a distinctively native game, was on its way.

A few blacks were playing on white college teams as early as 1890. Teams were organized at the early black colleges. Two of them in North Carolina—Biddle University and Livingstone College—played a game in 1892. Later, Howard and Lincoln, Tuskegee and Atlanta, Lincoln and Shaw—black colleges—established football and developed outstanding players.

And the blacks on white teams were beginning to attract notice. William H. Lewis of Harvard was chosen by Walter Camp, the patriarch of the game, as an All-America center in 1892 and 1893, and in 1900, when Camp named his All-Time team he again named Lewis. W.T.S. Jackson and Edward Gray starred at Amherst. Williams College produced George M. Chadwell, an end, and Ernest Marshall, a tackle. There were other Harvard stars, Howard Lee and Clarence Matthews.

Actually, though few blacks were able to go to college in those times, the ones who did, ran into little discrimination. Their number increased as football grew.

The early game was still marked by brawling play and little protective equipment, but there is no evidence that Afro-Americans suffered more wounds than anybody else. It was common for players to be led from the field with blood streaming from gashes on the scalp or forehead. Public disapproval grew into such an uproar that President Theodore Roosevelt called a White House conference involving the Big Three—Harvard, Princeton and Yale—to clean up the game and stop the carnage. The main change set up the line of scrimmage as it is known now, with no contact until the ball was snapped. Previously, opposing linemen had lined up head to head and there was always some merry scuffling before the play began. This often led to bloody slugging matches and officials had to pry combatants apart like boxing referees.

Cleaned up somewhat, football grew in popularity. Its peak point probably came in 1923, when the fabled Red Grange entered the University of Illinois and by his exploits pulled the game into the big time. Colleges began building stadiums seating 80,000 and 90,000 and alumni began paying muscular young men, with or without brains, to attend a particular university.

It is not likely that blacks cashed in on this benevolence. Those who did manage to get into a college, though, were welcomed by gridiron coaches, whose jobs were in constant danger if they did not come up with a sound football club. Blacks could not enter Southern institutions, of course, but in the North, Midwest and West Coast areas, their abilities were recognized and utilized.

Probably the first nationally known black to play college football was Brown University's fine end, Fritz Pollard. Son of a slave who had joined the Northern Army during the Civil War, Pollard stood only five-feet-six but was a versatile, exciting halfback. In 1916, he became a legend at Brown when on successive Saturdays he almost single-handedly defeated Yale and Harvard, when those teams were the most important and most powerful names in the business. Walter Camp named him All-America halfback that year and the Brown team went to the Rose Bowl in Pasadena, California, and Pollard became the first black to play in that historic series. One Pollard performance was described by a *New York Times* reporter this way: "(He) displayed the cleverest all-round backfield successes this year. In end running, forward passing, in executing a bewildering criss-cross and delayed pass run, in running back punts, in sidestepping and dodging tacklers in a broken field, Pollard gave a peerless performance . . . (that) brought the crowd of 25,000 spectators up with a roar . . ." (Later, as we shall see, Pollard became the first black in organized professional football and coached a major pro team.)

Walter Camp's earlier choice for All-America, William Lewis of Harvard, had become line coach at his alma mater after his graduation. Another Afro-American who became a major college line coach was Roy Young at Northwestern University in 1912.

By World War I, football rosters were well-dotted with black players. Remembered names include Edward Morrison at Tufts, Hugh Shipley with Brown University, Charles Ray who became captain of the Bates College team, Matthew Bullock, John Shelbourne and Leslie Pollard (brother of the great Fritz) at Dartmouth, and Joseph Edward Trigg who starred at Syracuse University.

Then Paul Robeson, who was to become a world-renowned singer, actor and student (and a controversial political figure because he said publicly that blacks would prefer the Soviet Union over the United States), burst upon the athletic fields of Rutgers University. He was a huge but agile man, son of a runaway slave who became a minister. Rutgers, at one time, acclaimed him as one of its five most prominent living alumni.

He won letters four times and was named by Camp and most newspaper polls as All-America in 1917 and 1918. He was equally adept on offense and defense. Against Fordham one year, he caught two long dramatic passes which spelled victory for tiny Rutgers, and his ferocious work on defense led to two or three Fordham men bei taken out of the play time and again. Robeson also was an outstanding debater, a member of Phi Beta Kappa, honorary scholastic society, and later won a law degree at Columbia.

As the Twenties came in for their roaring stay, sports in general took on a new eminence. Football was in the vanguard. Notre Dame's Knute Rockne became as famous, possibly, as the President of the United States.

And Afro-Americans drew their share of the limelight. It is hardly possible to name all the dark-skinned athletes who starred on the gridiron, so many became familiar in sports pages in all sections of the country.

Charles F. West was an outstanding halfback at Washington and Jefferson and played in the Rose Bowl. So did the University of Southern California's Brice Taylor (also an All-America), who though nominally a halfback, did the signal calling and play planning for the Trojans. Duke Slater, a bruising tackle, won All-America mention playing for the University of Iowa, and the two Simmons brothers, Ossie and Don,were among the five blacks on the Iowa squad.

In the Thirties, the black football star was no longer a novelty on college gridirons. There were few incidents, though on occasion Southern colleges tried to have blacks on opposing teams barred. Bill Bell, of Ohio State, had to sit out a game against Navy one year, but the following season State insisted that he take his place in the lineup. Syracuse's great passer, Wilmeth Sidat-Singh (who came from Harlem despite his East Indian name), was benched on purpose for a game with the University of Maryland. Dave Meyer, of New York University, was not allowed to play against Georgia. Washington and Jefferson held firm on playing Charlie West against Washington and Lee and it caused a break in athletic relations between the schools.

Levi Jackson with Yale coach Herman Hickman, 1949

But these were exceptions. For the most part, Afro-Americans were judged on their athletic skills. The University of Iowa elected Homer Harris as captain in 1938, the first black to be named to that post in the Big Ten. Indiana had a fine end in Archie Harris. The name of Willis Ward at the University of Michigan is well remembered, and Bernie Bierman's powerhouse Minnesota Gophers boasted a tremendous guard in Horace Bell. At the University of North Dakota, Fritz Pollard, Jr., son of the great Fritz of Brown, was worthy of All-America mention. The honored names piled up.

Brud Holland became the first black on Cornell's Big Red football team and is still listed as one of its all-time greats; he twice won All-America laurels as end. Kenny Washington, Woodrow Wilson Strode and Jackie Robinson were heralded on the West Coast for their superlative play for the University of California at Los Angeles. In the Midwest, Bernie Jefferson of Northwestern became a triple-threat wonder and often played the entire sixty minutes without being replaced.

Chester Pierce joined the Harvard team in 1947

45

After World War II, and a huge influx of blacks to colleges under the GI Bill of Rights, the list of stars became staggering. And rigid Southern bars against mixed white-and-black play were slowly coming down. In 1947, Chester Pierce of Harvard became the first black to play on a Southern college gridiron, against the University of Virginia at Charlottesville. Wally Triplett and Dennis Hoggard of Penn State played in the Cotton Bowl in Dallas, Texas, against Southern Methodist University. Kentucky State College, a black institution, played a white opposing team, Taylor University of Indiana, in a homecoming game. In 1949, Levi Jackson became the first black grid captain at Yale.

As the years rolled by, as in baseball, there was no question of a man's color, except in some extremely backward areas. The big names in college football rolled off the tongue of young and old alike without regard to race. Newspaper reports stopped saying "a black back."

Many of the college stars, who were to go on to professional play in many cases, left the campus life with glittering records and memories of pleasant Saturday afternoons deeply etched in the remembrances of college fans.

Just a short list of these collegians of football renown would include Bob Mann and Lennie Ford of Michigan, Ike Owens and Buddy Young of Illinois, Emlen Tunnell of Iowa, Linwood Sexton of Wichita, Bill Willis of Ohio State and George Taliaferro of Indiana. They were followed by Eddie Bell of Penn, J. C. Caroline of Illinois (who wiped out the total yardage record set by the legendary Red Grange), Bob Boyd of Loyola at Los Angeles, Lamar Lundy of Purdue, Raleigh Owens of Idaho College, Ollie Matson of the University of San Francisco and Joe Perry of Compton Junior College in California.

When the campus heroes left college, professional football seemed more enticing than other fields. Frequently the salaries offered in the beginning were not as high as those given to white men, because their bargaining position was often not as strong. Away from professional football, the work that awaited the black was nearly always menial and invariably low-paid. Football seemed better.

As their exposure and renown at college grew, blacks no longer had to approach the pros with hat in hand. They had talent and proved performances to show in their resumes. They could boldly rap at the door of professional football.

A master of defense, Emlen Tunnell was to reach prominence with the New York Giants during the late '40s and early '50s

74
90

CHAPTER VII

Football for Money

Pro football answered the knock on the door by throwing it wide open. From its beginning, the game never had raised much of a color line. Most professional players came out of college and in the early days not many blacks went to college. Thus, the ones who did, were exceptional and found no bars against them. There were occasional bigots, of course, who explained, as always, that blacks "preferred to play with their own," but through the years the pros never extensively degraded themselves with such nonsense. To be sure, in the early days blacks sometimes ran into rough treatment at the hands of opponents or fans. But as pros, the darker-skinned players could dish it out as well as take it, and their white teammates often did the job of "policing" the other side's roughnecks, if things got too dirty.

There was a pro grid black star as early as 1912. He was Henry McDonald, who first played at Canandaigua Academy and joined the Rochester Jeffersons, a team in a loosely organized league that was some years later to become the American Football Association, a forerunner of the National Football League. One of the Jeffersons' rivals was Jim Thorpe's Canton Bulldogs and one incident involving the teams may have set the pattern for the color barrier to remain down.

Henry McDonald, a hard-running halfback, found himself face to face with a Canton player not long removed from the South. The rebel, instead of trying to tackle McDonald, stopped dead in his tracks and drew back his fist. "Black is black," he said, "and white is white. Where Ah come from, they don't mix." McDonald also stopped dead and faced the white man. He happened to be a fine boxer, and he was prepared for action. But Jim Thorpe, the hero of the Olympic Games and certainly the

Jim Nance, of the Boston Patriots, plunges for yards against Houston greatest football player of his time, hurriedly broke up the encounter, growling, "We're here to play football. So let's play football." The game went on without further incident.

Some historians credit that simple move by Jim Thorpe as the basis for acceptance of blacks from then on. At any rate, eventually nearly every team in the early era had dark-skinned men on its roster.

They included some of the college greats, whose feats were described in the preceding chapter. Fritz Pollard, Brown's All-America ball carrier, started with the Akron Indians in 1919. He was also head coach of that team when it was still independent and not affiliated with the league that was organized the following year. But Pollard played for the Akron Steels in organized football, and later for the Milwaukee Badgers, the Hammond Pros and the Providence Steamrollers. One of his teammates on the Hammond club (National Football League, 1921–1926) was another Brown University star, one Jay Mayo (Inky) Williams.

Paul Robeson came out of Rutgers to play for Akron and Milwaukee before turning to the stage, and Iowa's All-America tackle, Duke Slater, played for a decade, winding up with the Chicago Cardinals in 1931. (Slater was easily identified from the stands, for he was one of the players of the time who played without a helmet.)

Oregon's Joe Lillard played with the Chicago Cardinals and the Philadelphia Eagles in the early Thirties, but many black college stars passed up the pros when they found color barriers in other fields beginning to crumble. It is also true that they found little encouragement in the later Thirties and in the war years.

It actually was not until 1946, after the Second World War, that black players began to flock into pro football in large numbers. One of the reasons was Branch Rickey's startling move in getting Jackie Robinson into baseball. Another was the formation of a new league, the All-America Conference, which began bidding for the football talent that had belonged exclusively to the old National Football League.

The new league, in order to provide topflight competition, needed blacks. One of its spearheads, Paul Brown of the Cleveland Browns—who had been quietly scouting players on service teams during the war—signed Bill Willis, an All-America lineman he had coached at Ohio State, and fullback Marion Motley, a star at the University of Nevada, whom Brown had known in Ohio high school football. They were both to become all-time pro greats.

In the old league, the Cleveland franchise had been moved to Los Angeles but the team still wore the nickname, Rams. Prodded by local fans who remembered the remarkable talents of Kenny Washington and Woody Strode when they performed at U.C.L.A., the Rams signed them, though both were well past their prime. Strode lasted a single season, but Washington worked valiantly for three years.

The dam broke with the signing of Willis, Motley, Washington and

Bill Willis, one of the first blacks signed to the All-America Conference

Strode and every team, with one exception, began seeking and playing blacks. The one holdout was George Preston Marshall, owner of the Washington Redskins.

Marshall continued to hold out and his teams suffered. By the time the two leagues merged after four years of fighting, the Redskins had settled down to being annual also-rans. They were never in contention for a period of more than a decade and finished last four times. Then in 1961, Marshall capitulated (mainly because he sought federal funds for a new stadium and could not get them, if he remained lily-white). He made a deal for Bobby Mitchell, a dazzling runner and pass-receiver of the Cleveland Browns. Mitchell led the league in catching passes the next year. The Redskins soon hired other blacks, and the team's play became respectable.

Meanwhile, every other football club in the pro ranks continued to add black players, and almost over night they became stars of the first magnitude. Marion Motley enjoyed unprecedented success as a piling, driving, indestructible fullback for the Cleveland Browns. In 1968, he became the first dark-skinned player to enter the game's Hall of Fame. Joe Perry of San Francisco was another outstanding ground gainer, both in the old A.A.C. and the N.F.L. Ollie Matson, from the University of San Francisco,

Number 89—Otis Taylor—in action against Miami

Marion Motley of the Cleveland Browns is tackled by Tom Keane, a back for the Los Angeles Rams

ground out yardage for four clubs in his fourteen-year big league career. The fabled Buddy Young caught on with the old New York Yanks and was the first of a long line of black speed merchants in the open field, who gave the fans countless thrills in the next two decades.

In 1949, when the All-America Conference gave up the ghost, three of its teams, Cleveland, San Francisco and Baltimore joined the National Football League. (After a fumbling start in Baltimore, that club, composed of players from the Brooklyn Dodgers, the New York Yanks and the New York Bulldogs, moved to Dallas. The club played there only for a year and then returned to Baltimore.)

Players from other A.A.C. clubs were put into a pool and chosen by the older N.F.L. teams. Among the selections were scores of black players who were to make headlines in the ensuing twenty years.

In 1960, the American Football League was organized and with the help of television subsidies maintained itself as a growing threat to the older National Football League—until 1966, when peace was arranged between the two. The first Super Bowl game was held in January, 1967, matching the winners, Green Bay in the N.F.L. and Kansas City in the A.F.L. Of the eighty players eligible for this World Series of Football

match, twenty-seven were black. Green Bay's Elijah Pitts scored two touchdowns for the winners, while Otis Taylor, a flanker from Prairie View A. & M., scored the Kansas City lone touchdown.

The exploits of Pitts and Taylor and the other blacks in the Super Bowl game represented something of a culmination of the efforts of hundreds of others who had followed Marion, Perry and Matson in the big pro game.

Over the years the list of Afro-Americans was more than impressive. It included, for instance, the man many people consider the best football player of all time—Jimmy Brown. When he quit the game in 1965, at age thirty-one, to act in movies, he was a legend in his own time. No movie script they could write for him in Hollywood was likely to match his real life story.

Brown was born on February 17, 1936, on St. Simon's Island, a tiny spot in the Atlantic Ocean just off the Georgia mainland. His parents split up when he was an infant and he was sent to live with his grandmother. At the age of seven, he rejoined his mother in Long Island, New York, where she was working as a maid. The requirements of her jobs kept her from keeping a close eye on Jim, and he grew up foot-loose and tough. He traveled with a rough gang which roamed Long Island streets looking for trouble.

The turning point in Jimmy Brown's life came when he began channeling his restless energy into athletics. At Manhasset High, he became one of the most versatile athletes the school ever had. He was befriended by a town lawyer who persuaded him to go to Syracuse University in upstate New York. And though Brown was not given an athletic scholarship, the friendly lawyer picked up the tab.

At Syracuse, things did not go smoothly. Brown stood six-one and weighed more than 200 pounds, but he was ignored by his football coach until well into his sophomore year. For one thing, he was the only black on the squad, and, for another, he was without a football scholarship, a highly suspicious state of affairs. Brown almost quit college, but he was becoming a stand-out in other sports (lacrosse, basketball, track) and this encouraged him to stay on. Actually, Brown said later, it was his R.O.T.C. colonel who talked him into continuing. When he was graduated from Syracuse, Brown was commissioned a second lieutenant.

But by then he had also become a fabled football hero. Stuck into the lineup at last, Brown became a spectacular ground-gainer and was mentioned for All-America honors by many experts. Following graduation, he was approached by the Cleveland Browns, whose rough and tough head coach, Paul Brown, offered Brown a $3,000 bonus and a first year salary of $12,000, quite high for a rookie and especially high for a black rookie.

Almost immediately, Brown began polishing his legend. As a rookie, he led the National Football League in rushing. He was named Rookie of the Year and was honored as All-Pro fullback, something rare for a first-year man. He was to go on and win the distinction seven more times and he was to be named Most Valuable Player on three occasions; nobody else has won MVP more than once.

Then in his second year, Brown really began making life miserable for opposing linemen and linebackers. He ripped off gains through the line that were remarkable. He ran the ends. He caught passes. He made the Browns one of the greatest of modern pro teams for the next nine years. Often he would be the key man (runner or pass receiver) for a dozen consecutive plays. In one game he was the key in thirty of the Browns' fifty-eight plays. Asked if he thought he was working his ace too much, Paul Brown said, "When you have a big gun—use it."

Jimmy Brown, in nine grueling years, set such remarkable standards that they may never be beaten. Eight times in those nine years, for instance, he led the league in rushing (second best is Steve Van Buren's four), and he carried the ball for an astonishing 12,312 yards (4,000 yards better than the second man, Joe Perry). He also scored 126 touchdowns (17 more than runner-up Lenny Moore). Once he got rolling, the Browns did not stint in paying him. He was earning $75,000 for football and another $50,000 as a radio man for a soft drink company when he decided to call it quits to get into movies. It came as no surprise to anybody that Jimmy Brown was an instant success in that field, too.

There were other important black players during the years Jimmy Brown dominated the offensive side of the game. There was Baltimore's Lenny Moore, out of Penn State, considered the most elusive back in the game during his eleven-year career. Once, a Washington Redskin defensive back, Ben Scotti, after having had to chase Moore all over the field one Sunday, remarked: "That guy is the toughest target in the league. He drops

The remarkable Jimmy Brown—he became a legend, setting records which may never be matched

his shoulder and bobs and weaves and doesn't give you more to shoot at. When you try to hit him, you only get a half of what you thought you were going to get."

One of the first blacks to gain prominence in the post–World War II period was Emlen Tunnell, who was a key man in the New York Giants' famous defensive unit of the late Forties and the Fifties. Tunnell, who had attended the University of Iowa, acted as free-wheeling safety man. He embarrassed every offensive back in the league. Not only was he able to intercept the opposition's passes, but he had enormous speed in returning the interceptions. One year he gained an unbelievable total of 921 yards on interceptions and kick returns—on defense. The ground-gaining champion on offense that year was the Rams' Deacon Dan Towler, and he gained only 894 yards. Prominent on the defense along with Tunnell, who later became the first black to become an assistant coach (with the Giants), were Roosevelt Grier and Roosevelt Brown. The latter, though nominally an offensive tackle, was inserted in the Giant defensive line when the other team got close to the goal. (Historian Robert Smith has noted: "A few centuries from now perhaps, if nothing remains to tell our story but the records of a few football games, it may be decided by record-diggers that a man named Roosevelt was a folk-hero of the American black, inasmuch as two men on the same team were named Roosevelt while records also revealed the name of a black named Jack Roosevelt Robinson. Who could say that these three were not all named after the same Roosevelt?")

Willie Wood, who came out of the University of Southern California to become an All-Pro with the Green Bay Packers, was another defensive whiz. He followed Tunnell, who had been traded by the Giants late in his career, and he was a worthy successor. He developed into a teeth-rattling tackler as Tunnell had been and was a superb punt-returner.

Wood, who had stood around street corners as a boy in Washington, D.C., could have got into deep trouble. But he found a friendly hand in a supervisor of a newly formed boys' club. The friendly hand, one Jabbo Kerner, arranged for him to go to high school, junior college and the University of Southern California. From there to the Green Bay Packers. Wood worked for years in the off-season with District of Columbia youngsters. He was their counselor and go-between on such matters as family, school and jobs. ("I can look at some of my boys," he once said, "and see myself a few years back.") Wood says that when he finishes football, he will devote his life to these kids. He feels that the personal satisfactions are great, though he also knows he could make more money doing something else.

Scores of superb black football players dotted the pro All-Star teams as the years rolled on. They supplied many of the thrills which resulted, near the end of the sixth decade of the twentieth century, in the pro grid game becoming so strong that it threatened to push baseball aside as the nation's national pastime.

The names tumble back: Big Daddy Lipscomb, Willie Galimore, John

Henry Jackson, Tank Younger, Inky Williams, Mel Triplett, Sherm Plunkett, Lenny Ford, Brady Keys, R. C. Owens, Willie Davis, Milt Davis, J. C. Caroline, Bernie Casey, Roger Brown, Kermit Alexander, John Baker, Paul Lowe, Lamar Lundy, Dick Lane, Jim Parker and many others.

Superstars in action—the Jets' Emerson Boozer and Joe Namath at the Superbowl, 1969

By the beginning of the 1968 season in pro football, there were 1040 players on 26 rosters, representing the getting together of the two big leagues. Of these a few more than 300 were blacks, a substantial 30 per cent of the total. And of those 300, an extremely high percentage represented the top-drawer talent of the game. Players of both the A.F.L. and the N.F.L. were polled before the season started to rate the best men at each position. Blacks fared well.

In the National League, Charley Taylor of the Washington Redskins was rated number one at split end; John Mackey of the Colts, tight end; Bob Brown of the Eagles, offensive tackle; Gale Sayers, Bears; Johnny Roland, Cardinals; and Timmy Brown, traded from the Eagles to the Redskins, best running halfbacks, and Leroy Kelly, Browns, fullback. On defense, David Jones of the Rams was chosen best end, with Willie Davis of

Green Bay a close second. The Packers' Dave Robinson and Herb Adderly were named best middle linebacker and best corner linebacker, respectively. Willie Wood, another Packer, was voted best safety man.

In the American League, players said Otis Taylor, Kansas City, and Al Denson, Denver, were the outstanding flanker backs. Walt Suggs, Houston, and Sherman Plunkett, New York, drew heavy support at offensive tackle. The best tight end was Willie Frazier, San Diego; the outstanding fullback was Jim Nance, Boston, while the three running halfbacks who drew the most votes were Mike Garrett, Kansas City; Emerson Boozer, New York; and Clem Daniels, Oakland. For defensive positions, Buck Buchanan, Kansas City, was named best tackle; Bobby Bell, Kansas City, best corner linebacker; and Butch Byrd, Buffalo, cornerback.

The road to this kind of acceptance by his peers has not always been a smooth one for the black pro football player. He has had to have extraordinary talent even to get a chance to make a team. Fairly good college players just are not approached by scouts. He has run into scores of instances of discrimination. Most people agree that there is an unwritten law on the number of blacks a club can keep and the number permitted on the field at the same time. (Something similar was true in baseball for the first half dozen years after Jackie Robinson broke the color line. Even Branch Rickey's Brooklyn organization would only field four blacks at one time. Eventually, as more outstanding black players came into the game, the rule was forgotten. The San Francisco Giants have used as many as eight non-Caucasians in a game.) In football, too, there is a general frowning on rooming whites and blacks together, though Green Bay's Jerry Kramer determinedly insisted on rooming with the Packers' fine safety man, Willie Wood, and the New York Giants roomed Gary Wood, a white quarterback, with Homer Jones, a black pass-receiver.

On some clubs white cliques sprang up. The St. Louis Cardinals one year had a particularly vicious set of racists who made things rough for the black players, apparently with the acquiescence of the white coaching staff. Black Cardinals reached the point where they petitioned the front office to fire one of the bigoted coaches. In Cleveland one year a golf tournament was held for the Brown football players but black members of the team were not invited, prompting a fracas during which one man said, "We black Browns are after the hide of this white Brown," meaning the player who organized the segregated tournament.

Blacks have other complaints against the football establishment. They seldom get the chance for endorsements and post-career jobs a white player does. Often, unless they are superstars, they are paid a lesser bonus and get lower salaries. They are many times patronized and considered kinky-headed mascots, or "fronts."

Then there is the question of the black quarterback. No matter how exceptional a black has been quarterbacking his college team, he invariably is switched to a different position. There never has been a regular

Roosevelt Grier (77) tries to block a Unitas pass

Roosevelt Brown (79), playing against the Packers, goes after a loose ball

black quarterback in the pro game, though a couple (Willie Thrower of the Bears, circa 1953; Choo Choo Brackins, Green Bay) were back-up men. Most often, the college quarterback sees the handwriting on the wall himself and changes his position before he reports to the pro club. He usually winds up as a flanker, a running back or a corner backer. For not only is he denied the quarterback position, he also is backed off from playing running guard or center. The white coaches' position seems to be that since the play starts with this little cluster of four men—center snapping to quarterback, guards blocking to one side or the other or pulling out to lead the play around end—that a black isn't capable of filling one of those spots.

As a result, the number of offensive guards on the twenty-six pro clubs can be counted on the fingers—and the number of centers—can be counted on one hand. But 90 per cent of corner backers are black because, the coaches seem to think, that position requires little judgment, only speed and the ability to stay with one man until the play is completed. The more complicated job is being middle line backer and deciding whether to go after the quarterback or try to knock down the pass. The implication that they can't exercise this kind of judgment also embitters black players.

Despite the bitterness, though, they admit that a good deal of progress has been made in twenty-odd years. There seems to be an easing of the strict quota restrictions. Half a dozen former black players have become assistant coaches. Segregation practiced in locker rooms and on airplanes is gradually disappearing. And, possibly most important, blacks with only medium talent are finding jobs, whereas in the past they needed superman ability. The New York Giants are grooming a black quarterback (Hank Washington) on their Westchester farm team. And when a white interviewer visits a locker room after the game, he is full of questions about the tricky move of an end or the faked field goal or the draw play that didn't work. The fact that the player is black or white does not count.

The most promising area of progress has come at Green Bay where the remarkable coach, Vince Lombardi, who became general manager, has had such success. Lombardi has insisted that the Packers be a family. "Black or white, you're part of the family," he announces on opening training. He has permitted no issue to arise about a man's color. If a bigot did appear in a Lombardi training camp, he was soon on his way. Black Packers have no complaints against Lombardi. And the team was compiling one of the most impressive records in football history.

Green Bay manager Vince Lombardi with Travis Williams

USA

CHAPTER VIII

Running and Jumping

Track and field, as organized sport, was dormant from the end of the ancient Greek Olympic Games through the Middle Ages. It is likely that small boys continued to race against each other during that period, for there is something basic about competitive running, jumping and throwing. But it was not until the nineteenth century that the first college track and field meet was held in England, pitting Oxford against Cambridge in 1864. Other European countries became interested in the sport and it spread across the Continent. The first formal meet was held in the United States in 1868.

Not long after that, the first black competitors appeared. They were college men. A man named W.T.S. Jackson ran the half mile in 2 minutes, 5.4 seconds at Amherst, respectable for the era. Napoleon Marshall ran the 440 at Harvard in 1895. Spencer Dickerson starred in many running events for the University of Chicago a year later.

No Afro-American athletes represented the U.S. in the first two Olympic Games, revived in Athens in 1896, and continued in Paris in 1900. But in 1904, the first black runner emerged in George Poage, an outstanding hurdler and quarter-miler, who had established a college record for the 440-yard race and for the low hurdles competing for the University of Wisconsin. The Games were held in St. Louis, and Poage finished fourth (behind three other Americans) in the 400-meters event, third in the hurdles race at the same distance, thus becoming the first black athlete to capture a medal in the Games. There were to be, of course, hundreds of others—gold, silver and bronze—in the Olympic Games to come.

Other notable track and field competitors around the turn of the century

Walking on air . . . long jumper Ralph Boston works out before the 1968 Olympic event

1914's "world's fastest human," Howard Drew—the first black to hold the title

were John B. Taylor, Howard Smith and Dewey Rogers, all from the University of Pennsylvania, and Ted Cable, who threw weights for Harvard. Taylor was considered on a par with Poage, the first black Olympian, at 440 yards and 400 meters. He was intercollegiate quarter-mile champion in 1904, 1907 and 1908, and once was clocked in the 440 in 48.8 seconds. (The record in 1968 had been reduced to 44.8 by San José State's black sensation, Tommy Smith, but considering that Taylor ran more than fifty years prior to that, the time was very good, indeed.)

Taylor was on the Olympic team in 1908, and reached the 400-meter finals along with two other Americans, W. C. Robbins of Harvard and J. C. Carpenter of Cornell. There was one Briton, Wyndham Halswelle, and the crowd, whipped up by London newspaper accounts, cheered him wildly and repeated the local sportswriters' warning that the Americans were going to gang up on him.

The four were closely bunched as they came around the last turn and entered the stretch. Robbins and Carpenter were neck-and-neck in front, the Englishman was third and Taylor, who had a fine finishing kick, was beginning to apply it. But Carpenter, meeting the Briton's challenge, swung wide—and British officials began yelling, "Foul! Foul!" One of the judges ran on the track in front of Taylor, who was trying to mount his big finish. Somebody cut the tape before the Americans could reach it and the officials declared the race void. They ordered a rerun for the next day, but United States squad leaders refused to allow Americans to run again on the grounds that the disqualification was not fair. Halswelle ran the course by himself and received the gold medal.

Six years later, in 1914, Howard Drew of the University of Southern California became the first black sprinter to be known as "the world's fastest human." He eclipsed the world 100-yard dash record with a spectacular 9.6-second effort that year. Earlier, Drew had been a high school sensation at Springfield (Massachusetts) High School and holder of the national Amateur Athletic Union 100-yard championship. He ran brilliantly throughout his college days, but because World War I canceled the 1916 Olympics, he never had an opportunity in that glittering international competition.

He drew his share of accolades, however. Mike Murphy, who had coached the 1912 American Olympic squad, watched him run one day and said: "Never in my life have I seen a sprinter with such wonderful leg action as Drew has. Why, his legs fly back and forth just like pistons. He gets away as fast as any man I ever saw, and he has a great finish." One track expert wrote: "It seems incredible that a man running without fear of life and not the slightest desire to catch a train can impel himself to such prodigious speed. The sight of Drew hurtling along inevitably suggests a concealed motor."

By the time the Olympic Games were resumed in 1920, Drew had retired to a career in medicine. (He was to make significant contributions in the field of blood plasma.) Other exemplary black athletes rose to take his place. Sol Butler of Dubuque was a premier broad jumper. The University of Chicago's Binga Dismond (who became a physician) was the best of a fine crop of quarter-milers. Others included William Hastie of Amherst, Charles West of Washington and Jefferson, Orthel Roberts of Iowa, Richard Moody of Marquette, Ivan Johnson of California, Harold Jewell of Northeastern and Cecil Cooke of Syracuse. De Hart Hubbard, who went to the University of Michigan, became a legend in the Midwest because of his versatility in the dashes, the hop-step-and-jump and the broad jump. Harvard's Edward Gourdin became the first man to broad-jump better than twenty-five feet, achieving the mark in a dramatic Oxford-Cambridge Harvard-Yale international meet at Cambridge, Massachusetts in July, 1921. Gourdin also won the national pentathlon championship. And though weight-throwing never has been a forte of black competitors, Thomas Anderson, representing the St. Christopher Club of New York, was acclaimed national Amateur Athletic Union title holder in the shot put.

The Twenties were years almost barren of records for Afro-American track and field athletes. As has been noted in other chapters, few blacks in any sport achieved recognition, or even opportunity, in that period. Historians believe it was because of a lingering backlash against Jack Johnson's period of high-living when he was world heavyweight champion of boxing. Whatever the reason, blacks did not burst out in full glory until the Thirties—and then they burst out with a vengeance.

By the time of the Los Angeles Olympic Games in 1932, names of blacks were in the headlines again. Eddie Tolan, a stubby little dash man from

Detroit, won the 100-meters in a photo-finish over another black, Ralph Metcalfe of Marquette University, who had been considered the favorite. Actually, the race was a dead heat, but the electric clock caught Tolan's chest a whisker in front of Metcalfe's. Then the next day, Tolan, his legs pumping like pistons, beat Metcalfe in the 200-meters. The chunky Tolan set Olympic records in both events. He went on from there to pile up a remarkable string of victories in amateur racing. In more than three hundred races, he was beaten only seven times. Later, Tolan raced professionally both in the United States and in Europe. Metcalfe returned to Marquette, where he captained the track team. Another Afro-American victory in the 1932 Olympics was chalked up by Eddie Gordon, of Iowa University, in the broad jump.

Other black dash men and broad jumpers followed. Besides the peerless Jesse Owens, who began making his mark as a high school phenomenon in Cleveland in 1933, the list included Ben Johnson, twice captain of Columbia University's track team, Eulace Peacock of Temple, Mack Robinson (Jackie Robinson's elder brother), Archie Williams and Jimmy Luvalle (quarter-milers), and scores of regional champions.

The domination of the shorter races and the broad jump by black competitors raised speculation in some quarters that they were peculiarly geared for this kind of running. Despite the fact that *no* Americans were prominent in distance racing beyond the mile, "scientific" treatises were advanced to explain the blacks' sudden success in track and field.

Dr. W. Montague Cobb of Howard University, a professor of anatomy, published the obvious disclaimer. Cobb pointed out that the American blacks being categorized in one lump did not even look alike. "Genetically," he wrote, "we know that they are not constituted alike. There is not one single physical feature, including skin color, which all of our black champions have in common which would identify them as blacks . . ."

But for whatever the reason, possibly an impassioned and fervid approach to training, black athletes continued to dominate many events. The international acclaim won by Jesse Owens for his superb performances in the 1936 Berlin Olympics (which will be detailed later) no doubt stimulated youngsters of his race to try to be like him. There were others to copy too: Cornelius Johnson of California and Dave Albritton of Ohio State finished one-two in the 1936 high jump. John Woodruff, a University of Pittsburgh freshman, won the 800-meters. Archie Williams, of Chicago, and Jimmy Luvalle, a Phi Beta Kappa man from the University of California at Los Angeles, ran first and third in the 400-meters. Owens, of course, came home with four gold medals in the 100-meter and 200-meter dashes, the broad jump and the 400-meter relay.

World War II interrupted Olympic competition for twelve years, but black track and field athletes were polishing their skills. John Borican, from Virginia State College, twice defeated the mighty Glenn Cunningham at 1,000 yards. Jim Smith of Indiana, co-captain of the track team, was a

Jesse Owens leaps 26 feet 5$\frac{5}{16}$ inches to set an Olympic broad jump mark, Berlin, 1936

27
46
226
120

consistently good miler. New York University's Jimmy Herbert set an indoor record at 600 yards. His teammate, Phil Edwards, held the half-mile record in the U.S. and ran third in the 1936 Olympics, though he represented Canada. A New York schoolboy, Frank Dixon, was an exceptionally able cross-country runner.

Among the broad jumpers were Kermit King, Pittsburgh (Kansas) Teachers College, who was national champion for a while; Bill Lacefield, University of California at Los Angeles; William Watson and Willis Ward of Michigan; Fritz Pollard, Jr., University of North Dakota, son of the All-America football player, and Ted Smith of Syracuse, Edward Brooks of Chicago, James Clarke of Indiana and Joe Batiste, a Tucson, Arizona, high school lad.

Performances in the high jump were similarly impressive. In fact, from 1932 to 1939 only one white competitor had even tied black high jumpers for the national Amateur Athletic Union title. Besides Cornelius Johnson and Dave Albritton, who ran one-two in the event in the 1936 Olympic Games, there were Mel Walker of Ohio State, Lloyd Thompson of Xavier of New Orleans, Albert Threadgill of Temple and Gilbert Cruter of Colorado University. The first man to clear seven feet was an Afro-American, Charlie Dumas, who also won a gold medal in the 1956 Olympics.

These were some of the early track and field stars, but black runners and jumpers in ever-increasing numbers came into the spotlight in the years that followed. In the flat races, there were dozens of names that won international acclaim: Barney Ewell, Bob Hayes, Andy Stanfield, Hayes Jones, Josh Culbreath, Charlie Jenkins, Mal Whitfield, besides hurdlers Harrison Dillard, Lee Calhoun and Hayes Jones. Whitfield, in 1954, became the first black athlete to win the James E. Sullivan Memorial Trophy, awarded to the competitor who "by his or her performance, example and influence as an amateur, has done the most for sportsmanship during the year." Later, Dillard, Rafer Johnson and Wilma Rudolph were similarly honored.

By the time of the 1968 Olympic Games in Mexico City, blacks had more than established themselves as an important group of Americans. There was a question, for a while, whether they would show up for the Games. But a threatened boycott was withdrawn, and when the final trials for the U.S. team were held, blacks were, as they had been for three decades, on the squad in depth.

They performed admirably. At Mexico City the U.S. won fifteen gold medals in track and field—ten of them (including our all black relay teams) by Afro-Americans. The fifteen first places were more than the U.S. had ever won before. The U.S. broke eight world records and tied another—all marks set by blacks. In running events up to the 1500-meter run, black Americans all but dominated the gaudy 1968 Games, which saw 7,226 athletes from 119 countries in competition.

But perhaps the most bizarre moment came when Tommy Smith and

Mexico City, 1968 . . . John Carlos breaks the tape in the 200-meter semi-final event

John Carlos, black sprinters from San José State College in California, ran one-three in the 200-meter dash final. They had run with knee-length black socks, signifying, they said later, their devotion to black people. Now they mounted the victory platform to get their medals from Lord Burghley, the Marquis of Exeter, who had been pressed into making the presentation. (Earlier, black Jim Hines, the 100-meter gold medalist from Oakland, California, and the third-place man, Charlie Green, also black, from Seattle, Washington, had expressed coolness at the idea of having Avery Brundage, the crusty old conservative who runs American Olympic matters, present their medals. So Lord Burghley was hurriedly substituted.)

Smith and Carlos walked to the victory platform, their hands behind them. Smith wore a black scarf, Carlos a black shirt. When "The Star Spangled Banner" was played, recognizing Smith's victory, both men raised black-gloved fists in traditional militant manner. They were barefooted and held their shoes in the other hand. They stared at the ground, rather than at the American flag. When they left the stand, they lifted their black-gloved fists once more. The Mexicans and the tourists in the huge crowd did not seem to know what was going on. Smith and Carlos tried to explain. "We—Tommie and I—would like to put in the papers some facts," said Carlos, the loquacious one of the two, at a press conference. "We think that white people feel that black people are nothing but animals. We got many boos out there today. White people turned thumbs down on us. We're not lower animals—roaches or ants or rats. If we do the job well, we get a pat on the back or some peanuts. And someone says, 'Good boy.' I've heard 'boy, boy, boy' all through the Olympics. I'd like to tell white people in America and all over the world that if they don't care for the things black people do, then they shouldn't sit in the stands and watch them perform."

The reaction was swift. The United States Olympic Committee held a frantic meeting and decided to kick Carlos and Smith off the team. The Mexican government revoked the pair's visas and gave them forty-eight hours to leave the country. The two blacks with their wives left immediately.

But things did not run smoothly, even after Smith and Carlos left the country. The other black athletes from America voiced protests, none loud enough, it seemed, to have them similarly ousted. Long jumper Bob Beamon (who had won his event with a fabulous 29-feet, 2½-inch leap) stood on the victory platform and displayed long black socks to protest, as he said, "what's happening in the U.S.A." Former champion Ralph Boston, who finished third in the long jump, took his shoes off on the platform and invited the Olympic Committee to send him home, too. Three U.S. runners—Lee Evans of San José, California, Larry James of White Plains, New York, and Ron Freeman of Elizabeth, New Jersey—who had wrapped up all three medals in the 400-meter final, appeared on the stand wearing black berets. The four black women who brought U.S. victory in the 400-

meter relay—Mrs. Margaret Johnson Balles, Portland, Oregon; Barbara Ferrell, Los Angeles, California; Mildrette Netter, Rosedale, Mississippi; Wyomia Tyus, Griffin, Georgia—said that they were dedicating their gold medals to Smith and Carlos.

In Washington, one Congressman (Representative John Conyers of Michigan) urged replacement of Brundage as president of the Olympic Committee. Secretary of State Dean Rusk said that his department was "inquiring closely" into the matter. The two black U.S. Olympic coaches—Pappy Gault of the boxing team and Stan Wright, an assistant in track—tried to calm down their charges.

Evidently they did, for the Mexico City Games ended on an even note and the United States again had demonstrated its superiority in track and field because of its black athletes.

CHAPTER IX

Five Great Ones

Jesse Owens undoubtedly was Amerca's greatest national track hero ever. He won laurels practically every time he drew on a pair of spiked shoes. A slender, almost fragile lad, he grew up in a Cleveland, Ohio slum, smashed running and jumping records at East Tech High School and became a national sports figure with his gaudy performances at Ohio State University. In his one glorious Olympic Games, in Berlin in 1936, he won four events—the only ones he was allowed to enter—eclipsed records in all of them, and did it against the fleetest and mightiest athletes of fifty-one other nations.

Owens's triumphs are all the more remarkable when viewed in the light of an impoverished background. He was born in Dansville, Alabama, September 12, 1913, son of a cotton picker and grandson of slaves. Early on, he knew how it felt to be so poor and hungry that potato peelings sometimes tasted good.

As a high school track wonder, Owens set a senior national A.A.U. broad jump record (close to twenty-five feet) and ran the 100-yard dash in 9.4 seconds, a school mark that has never been beaten in forty years. Despite his glittering performances, he was offered no athletic scholarship for college. He entered Ohio State at Columbus anyway and got a job running an elevator in the State Office Building. He worked from five to midnight, but found time to join the freshman track team. He set his first collegiate track record in the broad jump that year.

Then, as a 21-year-old sophomore, on May 25, 1935, James Cleveland Owens (his real name) was an Ohio State entrant in the Big Ten championships at Ann Arbor, Michigan. Against the nation's outstanding track and

field athletes, he did the following: At 3:15 P.M. he zoomed down the track to win the 100-yard dash and tie the world record of 9.4. At 3:25 P.M. he took his first and only broad jump and soared 26 feet, $8\frac{3}{4}$ inches, beating the world record by more than half a foot. At 3:45 P.M. he beat the rest of the field in the 220-yard event by more than ten yards, in the time of 20.3, a new world record. At four o'clock he won the 220-yard low hurdles in 22.6, taking four-tenths of a second off the previous world mark. In all, he smashed three world records and tied a fourth in a period of forty-five minutes. No other man, before or since, ever had such a phenomenal day from the time the first Olympics were held in ancient Greece.

Next came the 1936 Olympics in Adolf Hitler's Berlin. The Nazi Führer announced publicly that his white Aryan athletes would run away from blacks such as Jesse Owens. Instead, Owens performed so heroically and with such versatility that he left the sports world spellbound.

Owens exploded for his first gold medal in the 100-meter dash in the time of 10.3, an Olympic and world record. Then he leaped to another new Olympic record in the broad jump, 26 feet, $5\frac{5}{16}$ inches—truly remarkable in that no one had ever exceeded 26 feet before. He followed by winning the 200-meter dash by five yards over his nearest opponent and the record was 20.7, the fastest anyone had ever run the distance around a turn. Now, Owens led off for the U.S. 400-meter relay team, which also won, breaking the existing mark. The time was 39.8 for the four runners, an average of swifter than ten seconds a man for 100 meters. (Though no one has ever broken ten seconds in 100-meter sprints, relay runners, with the advantage of flying starts, have been able to average under ten.)

That performance dazzled the sports world. There were 893 track and field athletes entered, three times the number of preceding Olympics, and it necessitated many tiring preliminary heats. Owens had to run the 100 meters four times, the 200 meters four times, the 400-meter relay twice, and he broad-jumped twice. Of all the competitors, Jesse was the only one to win more than one gold medal.

He returned home to a hero's welcome, even a New York City ticker tape parade. He was hailed as the greatest Olympic hero of all time. He was admired the whole world over and traveled to many foreign countries as an American good will ambassador. In 1951, he returned to Berlin's Olympic Stadium and appeared in his track suit as part of a show arranged by the U.S. High Commission. More than 75,000 Germans turned out to cheer him, for many still remembered his incredible 1936 performances.

Later, Owens turned professional and raced against trucks and horses in exhibitions all over the world. Still later, he became secretary of the Illinois State Athletic Commission and devoted a good deal of his spare time to working with black youngsters.

But it is in track and field where he is best remembered. Not long ago, leading track and field coaches, experts and historians voted in a poll to determine the sport's greatest performer. The winner, overwhelmingly: Jesse Owens.

But perhaps the most dramatic upset in Olympic Games history was the one pulled off in astonishing fashion by a scrawny Ohio youth, Harrison (Bones) Dillard, in 1948. He won a gold medal in an event that wasn't even his specialty.

Born in Cleveland in 1924, Dillard was a child of poverty and grew up frail and undernourished. At the age of 12, he idolized Jesse Owens. Dillard wanted to pursue the sprints, but a coach in junior high school advised him to switch to hurdle races because the boy did not seem strong enough for the grueling sprints. Dillard became a hurdler, and he was an outstanding one—even unbeatable. At Baldwin-Wallace College in Borea, Ohio, he compiled a winning streak of eighty-two consecutive victories. It was a foregone conclusion that he would go to the Olympics as a hurdler.

But in the final trials for the Olympic team, for the first time in his life, Dillard knocked over a hurdle and stumbled. He straightened out—but knocked over the next hurdle, then another. Finally, he fell flat on his face. He lay there, clutching the cinders in shocked agony. The world's greatest hurdler had failed to make the team. He crouched in the middle of the track on his hands and knees, his hands over his eyes, and he cried unashamedly.

More or less as a lark, Dillard had entered himself in the 100-meter dash trials. He had won his heat, but he seemed to have little chance in the final, facing Mel Patton, the world record holder, and Barney Ewell, a three-time national sprint champion. Dillard finished a poor third, but at least he made the team.

There were sixty-eight sprinters entered in the 100-meters. To reduce the field, it was necessary to run off twelve heats, four second-round heats

Astonishing Wilma Rudolph races toward her second gold medal in the 1960 Olympic Games, Rome

and two semi-finals. Through them all, old Bones hung on, qualifying each time. On the big day of the final, Dillard faced Patton and Ewell and Panama's Lloyd La Beach, another champion. They were the three supposed to fight it out for the gold medal. The gun went off, and far on the outside in the sixth and last lane was Dillard, off like a rocket. On the inside lanes, the other three were locked in a fierce struggle. They gave no thought to Bones, far on the outside. They didn't even see him. At the finish Ewell crossed the line with a lunge. He knew he had beaten La Beach and Patton. He started to jump up and down with joy—until he saw the judges hailing Dillard as the winner. The world's greatest hurdler—a failure in his specialty—had achieved the most spectacular upset of the entire Olympics. And he had done it in record time.

Later, as Bones stood on the winner's pedestal listening to the bands playing "The Star Spangled Banner," tears filled his eyes. He was to say later that "it was the absolute climax of my entire life . . . I was living the greatest moment I'll ever experience."

Back home in the U.S., Dillard withdrew from sprinting almost completely and resumed his career as the best hurdler in existence. He beat all comers and when the Olympic Trials for the 1952 Games rolled around, he was ready. He won his spot on the team without difficulty. At Helsinki, Dillard showed his heels to the cream of the world's hurdlers.

At last he had accomplished what he had set out to do four years earlier—to win the Olympic high hurdles event. He skimmed over the barriers like a frightened deer. He again set an Olympic record.

Not long after the 1952 Games, Old Bones hung up his track shoes, quit hurdling and went into the business world. He was a successful and alert executive before very long and considered a community pillar. But track fans remember those two gold medals as evidence of his exemplary—and extraordinary—spirit.

The third of the greats was Wilma Glodean Rudolph. She won renown as one of the truly fine American track stars—and was often called "The Great Frozen Face." Her composure under the most harrowing of crises was remarkable, but it came naturally to her. Very early in life, she had courageously defeated overwhelming odds—odds that threatened her very survival.

She was born on June 23, 1940, in Clarksville, Tennessee, a sleepy tobacco town in the north of the state with a population of 16,000. Her parents worked in the fields and so did her many brothers and sisters as they grew old enough. She was the seventeenth child in a family of nineteen and weighed a little more than four pounds at birth. There was serious doubt whether she would live. And as she struggled for existence, amidst the prevalent poverty of that Southern state, she was struck with further misfortune. She caught double pneumonia, scarlet fever and, later on, polio, and the latter caused her legs to be paralyzed.

But Wilma's mother resolved that this infant was not to be lost. One day each week, the mother wrapped Wilma in a blanket and traveled ninety miles to a free hospital clinic. After years of medical treatment and long hours of daily massaging, Wilma's weak legs grew stronger and she was able to walk at the age of eight—with the aid of a leg brace. At thirteen, she was running like a normal girl of that age.

In grammar school and high school, Wilma emerged as a stand-out athlete. For five consecutive years, in her native county and in other parts of the state, she won every dash event in which she was entered, ranging from 50 to 220 yards. Her prowess spilled over onto the basketball court where she became an All-State player. In 1956, when she was 16, she scored 803 points in 25 games for her school.

At college she worked with more determination. She confided to intimates that she intended to become America's most famous woman runner. Though her friends encouraged her, most of them had doubts that a girl with such a crippling childhood ever would reach the heights. Wilma made it, though, and her performance in Olympic Trial competition established her as the outstanding U.S. woman runner. She easily qualified for the Rome Games of 1960. Still, there were doubts how she would fare against the world's top sprinters.

Miss Rudolph settled them quickly. She won her heats in both the 100-meter and 200-meter events. Then, against the best runners in the world, she won both finals, breaking the Olympic record at 100-meters and equaling it at 200. She topped those victories by running the anchor leg of the victorious 400-meter women's relay team, which also tied a record. She became the first American woman to win three gold medals in a single Olympics.

On her return home, Wilma Rudolph was lionized as the world's greatest woman runner. In 1961, she won the James E. Sullivan Memorial Trophy, symbolic of the athlete who best advanced the cause of sportsmanship that year. Though two women swimmers had earlier been honored, she was the first track and field female to be so applauded. And she was the first black woman to win it.

By the time of the Tokyo Games of 1964, Wilma decided she was past her peak and made room for other American women runners. They included Wyomia Tyus and Edith McGuire of Tennessee A. & I., in Nashville. Miss Tyus won the 100-meter dash in 1964; Miss McGuire, the 200-meter one.

Wilma Rudolph Ward (she was married in 1962) is the only American athlete whose likeness stands in the famed Madame Tussaud's Wax Museum in London. The wax model stares silently at visitors—its face composed, unruffled and cool. It is still the "Great Frozen Face." Visitors who know her record, however, say that she is entitled to a broad, beaming smile.

Number 4. Ralph Boston, a lanky, dedicated Mississippian, broke records that the experts said would never be broken. When the immortal Jesse Owens broad-jumped 26 feet, $5\frac{5}{16}$ inches in Berlin in 1936, many people said that this was the best that man could do. As for anybody reaching 27 feet, it was argued—that surely was impossible. It would mean, they said, that a man six feet tall would have to, after a running start, leap in the air and come down at a point more than four and a quarter times his own height laid end to end.

Boston proved the theories wrong. Just before the 1960 Rome Olympic Games, he leaped just three-fourths-of-an-inch short of 27 feet, breaking Owens's quarter-century-old mark of $26\text{-}8\frac{1}{4}$, the oldest record on the books. (Told about it, Owens's smile was a genuine one as he commented: "Ah, another old friend gone.") Then Boston went to the Games, broke Owens's record in that competition, returned home to jump past the supposedly unbeatable 27-feet barrier not only once, but many times.

The saga of this most remarkable of broad jumpers (or long jump, as it has become to be called) began in the mill-town of Laurel, Mississippi,

where Boston was born on May 9, 1939. He was "the baby" of a family of ten children, who were without a father. Their mother, Mrs. Eulalia Boston, worked as a housemaid to support the brood. Baby Ralph was a quiet one through his boyhood and did nothing much to attract attention until he made the track team in high school. He began making eyes pop then, for he broad-jumped 20 feet, 10 inches as a sophomore. He was outstanding in other events as well, and one time he took eight first places in a school meet. This versatility continued when he attended college, Tennessee A. & I. Boston was exceptional in the high jump, the hop-step-and-jump and in both low and high hurdles. In one meet he took first place in all of those events, in addition to his broad-jump specialty.

He easily leaped his way on to the Olympic team in 1960. On the eve of the broad-jump finals, Boston was chatting with Owens. "Jesse," he said, "you know how much I want to win that gold medal tomorrow. But there's a great field out there. To win it, I'll have to do something that may hurt you. I'll have to try my darnedest to beat your record."

Owens smiled broadly. "Ralph, I made that record a long time ago. I was twenty-three. Now you're twenty-one. It's your turn. Records are made to be broken. I want you to go out there tomorrow and fly."

Boston did exactly that. Though pitted against the world's best jumpers, three of whom topped twenty-six feet, Boston twice also went that far. But still needing a super jump on his third try, he sped down the runway, smacked the board and took off. ("He actually seemed to be flying through the air," an onlooker said.) When the jump was checked, it was the greatest mark in Olympic history: 26 feet, 7¾ inches.

Back home in Mississippi, Boston's aging mother was watching the event on television. She was so shaken by her son's performance that she poured herself a glass of milk and lay down to compose herself after the excitement. Suddenly there appeared on the television screen a picture of Boston himself. Remembering the years of sacrifice she had made for the family, Ralph endeared himself to millions of TV watchers when he held his gold medal aloft and in a moment of supreme happiness said: "Mom, if you're looking in, this is for you!"

There were later triumphs. He broke the 27-feet barrier in 1961 at Modesto, California, and again that year, in Moscow, he jumped 27-2 for another world mark. Four years later, again at Modesto, he set the unbelievable mark of 27-4¾ that was still standing as the Mexico City Games started in 1968.

Boston, if nothing else, had proved the experts wrong.

Winning the decathlon in track and field—ten widely disparate tests of speed, stamina, strength and spirit—needs the versatility and energy of a superman. Rafer Johnson, the six-feet-three California giant, in winning the decathlon Olympic crown in 1960, showed all those attributes—and more. He overcame serious injuries with tremendous courage. And he had to defeat his best friend to win the gold medal.

Johnson's dream of Olympic glory came early in life. He was born into a poor family in Dallas, Texas, one of six children. His father, a farm worker, moved his brood to Kingsburg, California, in the San Joaquin Valley, when Rafer was still a boy. The family lived in a railroad box car, converted into a house. But young Rafer withstood his impoverished background to become a high school athlete of some note. He led Kingsburg High to three football championships as a sensational halfback. He hit at a .400 clip for the baseball team. He was a star forward in basketball.

His real love, though, was track. He could do everything well. He confided to his high school coach that his dream was to become decathlon champion of the world. Johnson won a scholarship to the University of

California at Los Angeles. As a freshman decathlon performer he was impressive. He was at his best in the 100-meter, 400-meter runs and the shot put and discus. He had to work hard in the high jump, pole vault and broad jump. But he was such a promising star that his coach began grooming him for the 1956 Olympics at Melbourne, Australia. As that summer approached, however, Johnson aggravated an old football injury. He was not at his best at Melbourne and had to settle for a silver medal, second place behind another American, Milt Campbell.

At U.C.L.A. that year, Johnson met a young Chinese student, C. K. Yang, who had turned out for the decathlon after an exchange visit from Formosa. They became fast friends and trained together daily. No one could foresee that four years later they would be fighting it out for the Olympic Games decathlon medal.

Certainly the odds weighed heavily against such a proposition when, a year before the Rome Games, Johnson was involved in an automobile accident. He spent several weeks in a hospital with a severely injured back. He recovered sufficiently to enter and win the Olympic Trials, edging his friend, Yang. Both were named for the Olympics—Yang representing Formosa.

Rafer Johnson superhuman courage helped him overcome serious setbacks

Points in the decathlon events are based on a complicated scoring system, based on the time of the race, distance and height, plus the distance between the competitors at the finish, the world record for the event and many other factors. All the events are staged over a two-day period.

At Rome, the Chinese got off to a good start, beating Rafer in the 100-meter and 400-meter races. Johnson won the shot put, discus and javelin. Yang came back to win the 110-meter hurdles, high jump and pole vault. But Johnson had piled up enough points to lead going into the final event—the 1500-meter run. On past performances, Yang could take the title by beating his friend by ten seconds or more, a prospect not unlikely, since Yang had been clocked at 4:36.9, while Johnson had never bettered 4:54.2.

Both athletes were weary as they toed the mark for the metric mile. Both looked grim. They had been going at the top of their abilities for the past thirty-six hours.

At the gun, Fritz Vogelsang, of Switzerland, who was far behind in the total point score, jumped into the lead. The rest of the field stayed bunched. Johnson and Yang were close together. It was Yang's strategy to pull ahead of Rafer, but Rafer's plan of battle was to match his friend stride by stride for as far as he could. He hung on two yards behind as the race unfolded. Going into the last lap, the Russian, Yuriy Kutyenko, with no chance of winning the title, led and started to pour on the speed. Yang scampered after him. Johnson kept his cool and stayed on Yang's heels.

Now they swung into the home stretch, with still only a few strides separating Yang and Johnson. Rafer's weary-looking face was wreathed with a happy smile. He knew he had it made. And as he was mobbed by his American teammates, Rafer still smiled, though he showed compassion for the defeated Chinese lad. "I had to beat my best friend in the track world in the very last event to win," Johnson said. "Yang was tough and maybe he deserved to win. But, for me, this is something I've dreamed of for a long, long time."

When Johnson returned to his Valley home in Kingsburg, the natives turned out in huge numbers to greet him. Rafer was still smiling broadly. He remembered his long-ago dream when he vowed that he would become the best athlete in the world.

1948 . . . Harrison Dillard sprints to victory in the 100-meter Olympic event

LAKERS
13
DIEGO
11

CHAPTER X

They Came to Shoot

As the 1960's neared an end, black basketball players dominated the game. In the professional leagues, almost sixty per cent of the players were black. About half of collegian players were. The pro superstars, by their play for a decade or more, were Wilt Chamberlain, Bill Russell, Elgin Baylor and Oscar Robertson. Russell had been named coach of the Boston Celtics (the highest administration post in pro sports ever held by a black), and in the wings stood Lew Alcindor, destined to be the greatest of the great, once he was graduated from the University of California at Los Angeles.

It was not always so. In the beginning, blacks were barred from playing alongside white players. The game was invented by Dr. James Naismith, late in the nineteenth century. He was a physical education instructor at the Young Men's Christian Association in Springfield, Massachusetts. He used two peach baskets for goals. It was considered a sissy game at first, and few boys were interested.

But soon teams of basketball players were springing up all around the East. The Smart Set Athletic Club of Brooklyn may have been the first, followed by the St. Christopher Club of New York, the Jersey City Athletic Club, the St. Cyprian Athletic Club, the Salem Crescent Athletic Club and the Williamsbridge Colored Men's Association. Some, but very few, of these clubs played blacks along with whites.

In Pittsburgh, for instance, a team of white players won renown by beating all comers. It was the Coffey Club, named after Rabbi Jake Coffey. Though it had no black players, the Coffeys played against another Western Pennsylvania team, the Loendis—made up of all blacks. The Loendis and the Coffeys played each other five or six times a year for a six-year

Wilt Chamberlain reaches a little—and scores easily against San Diego

period around the time of World War I, trading victories of one-point or two-point margins.

In New York, a legendary team of whites, known as the Celtics and led by players such as Joe Lapchick and Nat Holman, was considered the best aggregation ever put together. It was called the marvel of its time. But a black club, the Renaissance team from Harlem, defeated the Celtics regularly when they were matched. Once, in 1938, the Rens played the Celtics before 25,000 fans in Kansas City—and gave them a sound beating. The players included Willie Smith, Tarzan Cooper, John Isaacs, Pop Gates, Puggy Bell, Eyrie Saitch, Zack Clayton (who was to become a big league boxing referee) and Fats Jenkins, a spectacular marksman, though he stood only five-feet-two. The Rens were so good that in sixteen years they won 1,588 games and lost 239. They swept through a professional tournament in Chicago without a loss. In Harlem bars, old-timers talk about the Rens as if they were still on the court.

Meanwhile, despite the excellence of the club and professional black basketball players, few with dark skins were making it in college. Coaches were reluctant to take the trouble of providing accommodations for black players on trips to the South. Often, they were left at home on such excursions. But some made their mark. Wilbur Woods played for the University of Nebraska as far back as 1910. Paul Robeson won his letter at Rutgers. The Reverend John Johnson was the first Columbia University black basketball player. Maynard Garner played center and was captain of the Hamilton College team. The Barnes boys, James D. and Samuel E., played for Oberlin. In the Midwest, Cleveland Abbott, Owen Ross and Horace Johnson were recognized stars, and in the Pacific Coast Conference there emerged a splendid Afro-American player, Ralph J. Bunche, who was to become a Nobel Peace Prize winner.

As the bars began to be lowered, other players won renown. Sidat Singh, an All-America football player, became an ace at Syracuse on the basketball court. Against Penn State, he scored eighteen points to lead his team to a 43–23 victory. (There were those kinds of scores in those days.) Said the *New York Times* man: "Wilmeth Sidat Singh has the canny sense of outguessing his opponents and that enables him to get a greater number of shots than do most forwards."

George Gregory, a one-time dropout from school, used his basketball mastery to attend DeWitt Clinton High School in New York. Later, he became basketball captain at Columbia. Dolly King played for Long Island University, under Clair Bee, and was recognized as one of the finest players of his time. Norman Skinner was a leading point-getter for Columbia. Ben Bluitt and Art White were outstanding at Loyola of Chicago. And after World War II, blacks came through as the best of the game.

One of these was Don Barksdale from the University of California at Los Angeles. Ten years after Jackie Robinson (who had been a whale of a U.C.L.A. basketball player himself), Barksdale was named a member

Syracuse's Earl Lloyd stretches his 6′6″ length to grab the ball away from the Knicks

11
NEW YORK
18
NEW YORK
17
3
11

New York Knick Cazzie Russell (33) streaks in to cover Elgin Baylor of the Los Angeles Lakers

of the All-Time Pacific Coast Conference team. He led the U.S. court team in the Olympic Games that year (1948), and the team did not lose a game. In fact, the American Olympic basketball clubs, manned by black players for the most part, have never lost a game in Olympic competition.

In 1949, professional basketball, which had been wracked by division, became an entity when the National Basketball League and the Basketball Association of America merged to become the National Basketball Association. Till then blacks had been ignored by the pros. But now, with Jackie Robinson making his dramatic debut in baseball, black players were sought.

The first to sign with the pros was Chuck Cooper of Duquesne University. The New York Knickerbockers engaged Sweetwater Clifton. The Syracuse Nationals named Earl Lloyd of West Virginia State as assistant coach and head scout. Soon, scores of blacks were dotting the rosters of big league basketball clubs. And the ones who emerged, were soon called the best in the business. One year, when an all-National Basketball Association team was named, four of the five players were black: Elgin Baylor, Wilt Chamberlain, Oscar Robertson and Bill Russell. Later, Russell became the first black to head a team in organized sports when he succeeded Red Auerbach as coach of the perennially champion Boston Celtics.

It was a move that figured. Russell had performed so valiantly for the Celtics that they had won their division title thirteen times in fourteen chances. Most people credited Russell. He was the first professional to play the ball instead of the man. While others watched their opponents, Russell kept his eye on the ball.

Russell turned the league around. He put glamour into defensive play and as that began paying off for the Celtics, others copied his style. His guarding tactics were so spectacular that for the first time in the history of basketball, people turned out to see defensive play. It became most apparent when Wilt Chamberlain, a scoring marvel, played against Boston.

Their first meeting, in the Boston Garden, is considered historic. Both men played the full 48 minutes. Chamberlain scored 30 points to Russell's 22, but this was hardly a victory for Wilt. Normally, in those days, he scored 45 or 50 points a night. Russell had 35 rebounds to Chamberlain's 28. The Celtics won easily, as they continued to do over the years when Russell played against Chamberlain.

Son of a foundry worker in Oakland, California, Russell attended McClymonds High School. He always said that he had a handicap—his older brother, Chuck, had been one of the best all-round athletes at the school. Bill shied away from sports until the basketball coach urged him to try for the team. He was only fair as a school player, but he showed enough to win an athletic scholarship at the University of San Francisco. His record there was astonishing. The team won fifty-five straight games. The stars were Russell and K. C. Jones, who was to become a renowned Celtic in later years. Bill Russell was hailed as Player of the Year for both of those seasons,

and once he attended a White House reception at which the nation's athletes were honored. President Dwight Eisenhower looked at the group and said: "You all look bigger on television—all but Mr. Russell." Later, Russell said: "Just imagine, with all those wonderful athletes there, the President noticed me."

After almost two decades in the game, Coach Bill Russell was still being noticed.

The other black man who revolutionized the game of basketball was Wilt Chamberlain, the seven-feet-one Philadelphian who went to college at the University of Kansas. There had been high scorers before Chamberlain (Elgin Baylor, the graceful sharpshooter for the Los Angeles Lakers, once scored 71 points in a game), but Wilt the Stilt, as they called him, casually overtook that record by scoring an even 100 points in his third year in the league.

It had been that way with Chamberlain ever since he joined the pros in 1959, the most publicized rookie of all time. There seemed to be no way to stop him. Bill Russell, who had more success than most against Wilt, once said, "I try to keep him away from the ball and try to stay between him and the basket." His questioner said: "What if that doesn't work?" Russell said: "I panic." Another time, Ed Macauley, who was coaching the St. Louis Hawks, said that he had his own defense against Chamberlain. "I will lock the dressing-room door before he comes out, and if that doesn't work, I'll use an ax on him." One National Basketball Association guard, assigned to disarm Wilt, said: "You hear a guy is seven-one and you nod. Then you face him on the basketball court and he looks like the Empire State Building."

No man has ever dominated one department of a game as Chamberlain has dominated scoring in basketball. Because of his amazing ability to get under the basket and stuff the ball into it, he is the greatest drawing card the game has ever known. One veteran sports writer has said: "In some ways he is the Babe Ruth of basketball. He is like the Babe in drawing crowds. And he is fabulous in his remarkable combination of size, strength, grace and speed."

It came as no surprise to anybody that Chamberlain followed Oscar Robertson of Cincinnati and Bill Russell into the Helms Hall College Basketball Hall of Fame. Russell was also given the Sportsman of the Year Award for 1968 from *Sports Illustrated.*

Though Chamberlain scored more points than anyone in history, perhaps the best black basketball player of all time was the sleek, flowing Oscar Robertson of the University of Cincinnati and the Cincinnati Royals. He was three times an All-America player in college, three times Player of the Year. Even so, he was subjected to humiliation when his college team was on the road. Once he was barred from staying with his teammates at the Shamrock Hotel in Houston. He threatened to take the first bus home to Indianapolis, Indiana. College officials made sure that he was properly taken care of after that. The team stayed in dormitories or fraternity houses for the rest of Robertson's college career.

Robertson was such an outstanding player on the court that he paved the way for other blacks to follow. Paul Hogue, Tony Yates and Tom Thacker all went to the University of Cincinnati solely because of their admiration for the Big O. They sparked the Bearcats to a N.C.A.A. title in 1961, and they unprecedentedly repeated the next season.

As a professional with the Royals, Robertson immediately became the idol of the fans. The club attracted more customers in the first quarter of the rookie year of Big O. than it had during the entire year before his arrival. One time he was hurt and missed four games—and not only did the Royals lose all four, but attendance dropped to practically nothing.

Wilt Chamberlain chuckles as he casually takes a rebound away from New York's Walt Bellamy

When he returned, he led the Royals to a victory over the Boston Celtics, something that hadn't happened in Cincinnati in three years, and, what's more, a full house was on hand to see him.

Robertson was enthralling. He stands six-feet-five, small for a pro player, but he was able to outjump anybody in the business. He has said he wants to be the perfect player. In that direction, he keeps his 195-pound physique in peerless shape.

Oscar was born in 1938 on his grandfather's farm near Charlotte, Tennessee. His father's grandfather, a one-time slave, was reported to be the oldest person in the United States when he died in 1954 at the age of 116. Robertson's closeness with the old man, it was said, had much to do with Oscar's acute awareness of his race.

14
44
16

When he was four, his parents took him and his two older brothers to live in Indianapolis. His father left home not long thereafter. His mother worked to raise the children. Oscar was determined to repay her, and he did when he became a professional player. After attending an all-black high school, Crispus Attucks, he got offers from many colleges. (Even Adolph Rupp, coach of Kentucky, offered him a scholarship, and Kentucky had never had a black basketball player.) He chose Cincinnati partly because it was near home and partly because it had a cooperative work plan. He worked his way through. In 1960, he and Jerry West co-captained the undefeated U.S. Olympic basketball team.

Robertson's personal hero was Jackie Robinson. "He did something few of us could have done," he once said. "He took a terrible beating for the sake of a principle, and all of us gained by it. Every black in America owes him a debt of gratitude. I'd give anything to be like him."

Most people think Robertson has been, indeed, very much like Jackie Robinson.

Cincinnati Royals' ace Oscar Robertson (14) in action

CHAPTER XI

Golf and Tennis and Stuff Like That

"The golf links
lie so near the mill
That almost every day
The laboring children can look out
And watch the men at play."

Sarah Cleghorne's acid lines on child labor could as easily have been applied to blacks who aspired to play golf. Organized golf was one of the last games to eliminate segregation, and though there were fine black players, they were generally limited to their own courses playing against other blacks. In fact, it was not until 1967, that a black won a Professional Golfers Association tournament; Charlie Sifford at Hartford, Connecticut.

Golf dates back to the fourteenth century and originated in Holland or Scotland, depending on which history book you read. It had its origins in America in 1888, when a Scot, John G. Reid, organized the St. Andrews Golf Club of Yonkers, New York. In 1894, the U.S. Golf Association was founded to govern the game and conduct annual tournaments, the National Amateur and the National Open (for both professionals and amateurs). The pros got their own organization, the P.G.A., in 1916. Through all the beginnings, however, black players, for the most part, were on the sidelines.

Black youngsters were introduced into the game as caddies, and many of them developed into quite able golfers. Occasionally the exclusive clubs would hold "caddy" matches when blacks were permitted to show their stuff. But discrimination held on tenaciously until the late 1950's. Even then,

Charlie Sifford follows his shot

representation was token. No black, for instance, ever has qualified for the Masters held annually in Augusta, Georgia. But since 1926, blacks have been able to compete in tournaments sponsored by the United Golfers Association, which holds yearly National Open and National Amateur events.

One who did break through was John Shippen, who probably was the first golf club pro in the U.S. born in this country. The other club pros were imported from Scotland and England. But around 1900, Shippen and his brother, Cyrus, instructed on some of the exclusive courses in the East and often played exhibition matches with many famous golfers.

John was the first black to enter the U.S. Open, in its second year in 1896. Just eighteen, Shippen drew some objections, but Theodore Haverman, president of the U.S.G.A., stood firm and said that unless Shippen played, he would call the tournament off. Shippen finished fifth. He defeated a stockbroker named Charles MacDonald by five strokes, and MacDonald was one of the big names in golf, having won the first U.S. Amateur title the year before. On the final tee, Shippen drove 175 yards, a mighty blow for the time, and as caddies mobbed him, MacDonald went off in a huff and quit the tournament. One sports writer said: "Shippen, all things considered, is the most remarkable player in the country." Shippen continued to instruct golf until his retirement. Then he went to a nursing home, on welfare funds, and died, at age ninety, in 1968.

There were black U.S.G.A. champions over the years, but after Shippen, no prominent black golfer came through in white tournaments until Charlie Sifford in the Fifties. A former caddy, Sifford was so good that he was able to break color bars in some areas of the South, including his native North Carolina and Texas. In 1957, he became the first black to win a big-time Open, the Long Beach, when he defeated Eric Monti in a sudden-death playoff. Ten years later he won at Hartford, Connecticut, against the best professionals.

Earlier, though, despite the advancement of black players, they were generally kept from entering tournaments. In 1947, the Richmond, California, Open officials barred two fine blacks, Bill Spiller and Ted Rhodes, both of whom had qualified in the Los Angeles Open. Other early outstanding golfers, who made their names in black tournaments or in college play, included Pat Ball, John Dendy, Solomon Hughes, Zeke Hartsfield, A. D. V. Crosby, Howard Wheeler, George Roddy (one-time captain of the Iowa State College team) and Harry Jackson (winner of the inaugural professional black national tournament).

As the civil rights movement increased in tempo after World War II, many advances were recorded, particularly after the Supreme Court desegregated schools in 1954. Blacks, over great obstacles, won the right to play on municipally owned courses. Where there were separate courses for blacks, some court decisions declared that the facilities were "not substantially equal" to the ones provided for whites. Many blacks carried the fight by showing up to play on previously restricted public courses. Finally, in 1955, the Supreme Court ruled that segregation of races was illegal on public golf courses.

By 1959, Bill Wright, from Kansas City, Missouri, a student at Western Washington College, won the National Public Links Golf Champions—the Standish Cup. It was the first time a black ever won a major public links tournament. (Wright's father was a mailman, who also entered the qualifying Publinks round at Seattle, and in order to win his own berth, Bill Wright had to defeat his father.)

One of the great black golfers to emerge in the late 1960's was Lee Elder, who at age 33 came out of Dallas, Texas, to finish second to one of golf's mightiest players, Jack Nicklaus, in the American Golf Classic at Akron, Ohio. One year Elder played in eighteen P.G.A. tournaments, finishing in the money in fourteen of them. His earlier claim to fame was, when he was sixteen, playing Joe Louis for the title in the United Golfers Association finals in 1950. ("Actually, I wasn't quite sixteen," Elder explained much later. "But I would have had to play against kids, so I fibbed a little.")

Elder's success portends advancement for black golfers for the future, even though the game has lagged behind most other sports in the drive to destroy the color line.

When Lieutenant Arthur Ashe became the first black to become the U.S. men's amateur tennis champion, in 1968, he remarked with some wryness:

"Funny thing. My color would bar me from membership in seven-eighths of the clubs where I play my matches." As if to confirm his words, a few days later an exclusive Washington, D.C. country club, Chevy Chase, refused to book tennis matches with rival clubs which had black members.

A small furor ensued but died down in a few days, as it had for all the years clubs enforced lily-white policies since the beginning of tennis in America. Tennis, like golf, was very late indeed in catching on to the great social changes taking place. Even as late as the 1960's, color lines were still being drawn. As a result, many country clubs were losing influential members, such as Richard Nixon, the late Robert Kennedy, former New York City Mayor Robert Wagner and countless theater and movie stars.

Ashe was a remarkable exception. He had become the first black player on the Davis Cup squad. He followed his triumph in the amateur men's singles by winning the first United States Open tennis championship, in which both professionals and amateurs competed—and doing it in such convincing fashion that tennis writers were predicting that he would be at the top of the heap for years to come. His road to that double victory had not been an easy one. Born in Richmond, Virginia, in 1943, he found he could not play at the "whites only" recreation park, but was shunted off to the courts for blacks in another park. He started playing there with a borrowed racket, played segregated tennis most of the time, then won a scholarship to the University of California at Los Angeles. He became National Collegiate champion, then won appointment as a West Point cadet, got his second lieutenant's bars and continued to play spectacular tennis. Once after he had been to Australia and had won four tournaments, the mayor of Richmond proclaimed an "Arthur Ashe Day." Ashe, witty and knowing, smiled at the notion, remembering that only ten years earlier he had been barred from playing on Richmond's white public park courts.

In the beginning, there were no such success stories. Tennis was introduced to this country in 1873, when the game caught on in New England, New York City and California. In 1881, the United States Lawn Tennis Association was formed and the first U.S. singles tournament was conducted, naturally without black participants. Six years later the first U.S. singles tournament for women was held. It was also all-white.

For many years tennis in the United States was considered a rather sissy game and drew only the elite. It remained almost exclusively a rich man's amateur sport until 1926, when Suzanne Lenglen of France, a redoubtable court champion, turned professional. She accepted $50,000 from sports promoters named Cash and Carry Pyle and toured the country with Mary Brown, Vincent Richards and Howard Kinsey. The U.S. Professional Lawn Tennis Association was organized in 1927. But amateurism still held sway and professionals and amateurs never met in one tournament until late 1968.

In the early days some interest among blacks was evinced for the new game. It became popular in some all-black colleges, and among the prominent early champions were Warren Logan, Emmett J. Scott, S. E. Courtney and E. T. Attwell, all of Tuskegee; Thomas Jefferson, of Lincoln University; Charles Cook of Howard University; the Reverend W. W. Walker, of the Chautauqua Tennis Club, and Walker's protégé, Edgar G. Brown, a daring innovator who turned the game around with his colorful, dashing style of play. Scores of black tennis clubs began springing up throughout the country. In 1916, faced with the same segregation that golfers had to put up with, black tennis players organized the American Tennis Association, aimed at fostering and developing the game among the black people of the country. At the first national tournament in Baltimore's Druid Hill Park, Talley Holmes and Sylvester Smith were crowned national champions.

Lee Elder was one of the few black golfers of the early '50s

Arthur Ashe faced countless obstacles, but kept his sense of humor—and his determination

Many strong college players developed as well. Richard Hudlin was captain of the tennis team at the University of Chicago. Doug Turner was a letter man at the University of Illinois. In the East, Reginald Weir, of City College of New York, and Gerald Norman, Jr., were both rejected for the national indoor championships because of their color.

Remarkable women players were developing, too. One, Ora Washington of the Germantown YWCA in Philadelphia, was probably most outstanding. She played tennis for twelve years without being defeated and she won 201 trophies. Her chief rivals included Emma Leonard, Frances Giddens and Lillian Hines, but they were overmatched against Miss Washington's blazing serve and all-round game. Her big dream was some day to play against Helen Wills Moody, then queen of the courts, but Miss Moody avoided Miss Washington's challenges for many years. Flora Lomax of Detroit followed Ora as women's black champion and taunted her to come out of retirement. Ora did and trounced Miss Lomax with authority. Another Philadelphia tennis whiz was Inez Patterson, who excelled in many sports.

The most spectacular black woman athlete was yet to come. She was the stunningly professional Althea Gibson, who came out of the streets of Harlem to become the foremost woman athlete of her time. As a young tomboy, she fought, played baseball and football and tried her hand at "paddle-ball," a sort of ping-pong. She quit high school, worked as a counter girl at Chock Full O'Nuts, as a runner for a blueprint company, as a button maker in a factory and as an elevator operator in the Dixie Hotel.

By the time she was eighteen, she knew her way around and she had begun to play tennis. She was befriended by Sugar Ray Robinson, the fight champion, and his wife, and she credited them with much of the glory that followed. Then she became a protégé of two tennis-playing doctors, Dr. Hubert A. Eaton of Wilmington, North Carolina, and Dr. Robert W. Johnson, of Lynchburg, Virginia. She began winning tournaments, not only black ones but also against white women.

They were not easy years for Althea, coming up as challenger to the great players of the world. But she worked hard, won her share of titles and became the first black woman to compete in the National Indoor championships. She lost in the quarter-finals. In the Forest Hills grass court championships, she was defeated by Louise Brough, national and Wimbledon champion. She went to Mexico City, Paris, Southeast Asia. Then in 1956, at Wimbledon, she lost to Shirley Fry. She lost again to Miss Fry at Forest Hills.

Then it all came together for Althea Gibson. In 1957, in July, she won the Wimbledon title, beating Darlene Hard of San Diego, California. Now she was the first black international champion tennis had ever seen. And in September, in the national women's singles final at Forest Hills, she conquered Louise Brough in straight sets. She won all the honors. The Queen of England presented her with the Wimbledon Cup. Vice President Richard Nixon shook her hand when she won the nationals' crown. President Eisenhower wrote his congratulations. Althea wore her honors well. She later became a night club singer and a champion woman golfer. She had help from friends, but she did a good deal of it by herself. The odds were never in her favor. From 143rd Street in Harlem to the center court at Wimbledon is about as far as one can travel.

When the news came on the radio that Althea had won the Wimbledon Cup, her mother and father sat in their Harlem apartment with sports writer Milt Gross. "I didn't think she'd make it," her mother said. "I mean —a black girl going that high." Her father said: "I knew she'd do it. She only wanted to try for the top. I knew she had the strength to do it." "What kind of strength do you mean?" Milt Gross asked. "Physical strength— and any other kind of strength that's needed," said Althea Gibson's father.

This book has only skimmed the surface of black participation in athletics. In the dozens of other of the myriad sports that make up the American scene, blacks have been taking their places—perhaps not in the

Congratulations for Althea Gibson, Wimbledon Singles champ, from her defeated opponent, Darlene Hard. Althea holds the trophy presented to her by Queen Elizabeth

proportion they have in the major ones, but taking their places, nevertheless. (In many cases, lack of facilities over the years held blacks back. They first became best known in sports that required inexpensive gear. That may be changing in the years ahead.)

Still, there are few sports whose records aren't at least sprinkled with outstanding black Americans. Rojo Jack was an outstanding auto racer, though he never drove in the Indianapolis 500. Joe Ray, Jr., was another auto racer. Marshall (Major) Taylor was a champion bicycle rider at the turn of the century and three times won American sprint titles. In college wrestling, Walter Gordon, of the University of California, once was heavyweight champion of the Pacific Coast. The first black to race in varsity crew was Joe Trigg at Syracuse University in 1915. Richard Henry captained the Northeastern University fencing team in the Twenties. There have been countless champion bowlers since that sport became a major U.S. recreation, though it took a major battle to break the "Caucasians only" rule of the American Bowling Congress in the 1950's. Ice hockey, lacrosse, skiing, and archery are among the other sports which have seen the emergence of the black athlete, sometimes, to be sure, in the slowest of fashion.

Althea Gibson, intently working toward her victory over Australia's Mary Heller, Wimbledon, 1957

CHAPTER XII

What Now?

Back in the 1940's and 1950's—when there were enough newspaper jobs to go around—this author was a sports writer traveling with the New York Yankees. Once, on the way home from spring training, we got into Louisville, Kentucky, for an exhibition game, one of a series of daily stands that used to feature the end of training. As the bedraggled Yankee party stumbled out of cabs at 6:00 A.M. in front of the Brown Hotel where we were to stay, we ran into a picket line. It was manned mostly by black bellmen and maids, who were on strike, their signs said, to raise wages above the prevailing scale of twenty cents an hour. I chose not to go through the line, mainly, I suppose, because I feared that if I did, my father—a militant trade union man from the Clydeside shipyards in Scotland—would hear about it. All the other people with the Yankees—players, coaches, trainers, hangers-on, announcers and sports writers from liberal papers—sailed right through. (I wrote my story that day on a portable in my lap at Union Station. I had called Casey Stengel, the manager, to explain why I couldn't be at his press conference. Casey said that he understood, and, in fact, gave me a pretty good story.)

I recall this incident only to suggest that it would probably not happen today—two decades later. This is not to say that the pickets would be hailed as soul brothers by the arriving athletes, but that the momentum produced by the nation's struggle to achieve social and economic justice has spilled over into the once-insulated world of sports. Actually, gains made by blacks in sports have far out-distanced gains in other fields. Even if, as is probable, the sports establishment was motivated by economic factors (black patrons buy box seats, too), it has often been ahead of the rest of

Ralph Bunche, today the Under-Secretary General of the United Nations, enjoyed sports while in college the nation. And, more important, it has given fulfillment and wealth and education to thousands of players. Most of it happened in the two decades mentioned.

For instance, there was no Jackie Robinson in baseball's Hall of Fame. Roy Campanella, Willie Mays, Ernie Banks, Frank Robinson, Elston Howard, Hank Aaron, Lou Brock, Bob Gibson, and other heroes, had not arrived on the scene. Neither had Jimmy Brown in football, nor Willie Galimore, O. J. Simpson nor Leroy Keyes. Wilt Chamberlain had not sprung forth either, or Bill Russell, Lew Alcindor, in basketball. Nor had Rafer Johnson, Ralph Boston, Tommy Smith, in track. And Wilma Rudolph and Althea Gibson had still to win their honors in track and tennis, respectively, as Sports Women of the Year. It would have been hard to imagine a black umpire in the major leagues (Emmett Ashford). It would have been hard to expect a big league coach (Jim Gilliam of the Los Angeles Dodgers). It would have been inconceivable to believe that Maury Wills and Bill White, ballplayers, would be seriously considered for major league managing jobs. And it would have been difficult to contemplate that Monte Irvin would be named to an important post as assistant to Commissioner of Baseball William Eckert—the first black to achieve any kind of recognition in the baseball hierarchy.

Most unlikely of all would have been the prospect of functioning players' associations in major sports, putting forth demands for minimum salaries and better conditions and more of a voice in running the organization. And even, in the case of the Olympic black rebels, demanding that the heavyweight title stripped from Muhammad Ali be returned to him. "A boycott of the Olympics by its best black athletes," one said, "would give many pause to evaluate their own goals. And it would jolt the country into taking more positive steps toward improving housing, education and job opportunities for black Americans." As it turned out, the boycott was abandoned—but the spirit remained.

The basic point is that sports in America has reversed its stand on the question of black players. There are still gains to be made. They will be made against a background of tumultuous activity in the nation in other fields. But they will be made.

BIBLIOGRAPHY

Allen, Lee, *The Hot Stove League,* Barnes, 1955.

———, *The National League Story,* Hill and Wang, 1961.

Ashe, Arthur, *Advantage Ashe,* Coward-McCann, 1968.

Auerbach, Arnold (Red), with Paul Sann, *Winning the Hard Way,* Little Brown, 1966.

Bisher, Furman, *With a Southern Exposure,* Nelson, 1962.

Breslin, Jimmy, *Can't Anybody Here Play This Game?,* Avon, 1963.

Brown, Jimmy, *Off My Chest,* Doubleday, 1965.

———, "My Roommate," article, *Sport* Magazine, December, 1965.

Daley, Arthur, *Pro Football's Hall of Fame,* Quadrangle Books, 1963.

Davis, Mac, *100 Greatest Sports Feats,* Grosset and Dunlap, 1964.

Donovan, Richard, "The Fabulous Satchel Paige," article, *Collier's,* 1953.

Durant, John, *Highlights of the Olympics,* Hastings House, 1965.

Fleischer, Nat, *Ring Record Book,* annual.

Garagiola, Joe, *Baseball Is a Funny Game,* Lippincott, 1960.

Gibson, Althea, with Ed Fitzgerald, *I Always Wanted To Be Somebody,* Harper and Bros., 1958.

Gregory, Dick, with Robert Lipsyte, *nigger,* Dutton, 1964.

Hand, Jack, *Heroes of the NFL,* Random House, 1965.

Hano, Arnold, *A Day in the Bleachers,* Crowell, 1955.

Heinz, W. C., "I Remember Boxing," article, *Sport* Magazine, 1961.

Hirshberg, Al, *Russell of the Celtics,* Messner, 1963.

———, *Basketball's Greatest Stars,* Putnam's, 1963.

———, *Basketball's Greatest Teams,* Putnam's, 1964.

Isaacs, Stan, *Careers and Opportunities in Sports,* Dutton, 1964.

Kahn, Roger, "The Ten Years of Jackie Robinson," article, *Sport* Magazine, 1955.

Kieran, John and Daley, Arthur, *The Story of the Olympic Games,* Lippincott, 1957.

Klein, Larry, *Jim Brown, the Running Back,* Putnam's, 1965.

Koppett, Leonard, *A Thinking Man's Guide to Baseball,* Dutton, 1967.

Krout, John A., *Annals of American Sport,* Yale University Press, 1929.

Lardner, John, *It Beats Working,* Simon and Schuster, 1951.

Mann, Arthur, *Branch Rickey,* Houghton Mifflin, 1959.

Mann, Jack, *The Decline and Fall of the New York Yankees,* Simon and Schuster, 1967.

Meany, Tom, *Baseball's Best,* Watts, 1964.

———, *There've Been Some Changes in the World of Sports,* Nelson, 1962.

Menke, Frank, *Sports Tales and Anecdotes,* Barnes, 1953.

———, *The Encyclopedia of Sports,* Barnes, 1963.

Newcombe, Jack, *The Fireside Book of Football,* Simon and Schuster, 1964.

Olsen, Jack, *The Black Athletes: A Shameful Story,* Time-Life Books, 1968.

Orr, Jack, *Baseball's Greatest Players Today,* Watts, 1962.

———, "Jackie Robinson—Symbol of the Revolution," article, *Sport* Magazine, 1960.

Reichler, Joe and Olan, Ben, *Baseball's Unforgettable Games,* Roland, 1960.

Paul, C. Robert and Jack Orr, *The Olympic Games,* Lion Press, 1968.

Rice, Grantland, *The Tumult and the Shouting,* Barnes, 1959.

Rickey, Branch, with Robert Riger, *The American Diamond,* Simon and Schuster, 1965.

Ritter, Lawrence S., *The Glory of Their Times,* Macmillan, 1966.

Robinson, Jackie, with Wendell Smith, *Jackie Robinson,* Greenberg, 1948.

———, with Charles Dexter, *Baseball Has Done It,* Lippincott, 1964.

Sackler, Howard, *The Great White Hope,* Dial, 1968.

Schaap, Dick, *The Olympic Games,* Simon and Schuster, 1964.

———, "The Mixed Emotions of 'The Big O'," article, *Sport* Magazine, 1959.

Seymour, Harold, *Baseball: The Early Years,* Oxford University Press, 1960.

Shapiro, Milton J., *The Willie Mays Story,* Messner, 1960.

Smith, Ken, *Baseball's Hall of Fame,* Barnes, 1952.

Smith, Red, *Views of Sport,* Knopf, 1954.

———, *The Best of Red Smith,* Watts, 1963.

Smith, Robert, *Baseball in America,* Holt Rinehart, 1961.

———, *Pro Football,* Doubleday, 1963.

Sport Magazine: "The Negro in Sports," special issue, March, 1960.

Treat, Roger, *Official Encyclopedia of Football,* 5th Revised Edition, Barnes, 1967.

Turkin, Hy and Thompson, S. C., *Official Encyclopedia of Baseball,* 5th Revised Edition, Barnes, 1967.

Unitas, Johnny, with Ed Fitzgerald, *Pro Quarterback: My Own Story,* Simon and Schuster, 1965.

Veeck, Bill, with Ed Linn, *Veeck as in Wreck,* Putnam's, 1962.

Young, A. S. (Doc), *Great Negro Baseball Stars,* Barnes, 1953.

———, *Negro Firsts in Sports,* Johnson Publishing, 1963.

INDEX

A

B

C

D

E

F

G

H

I

J

K

L

M

N

O

P

Q

R

S

T